HEROIC ANIMALS

TRAKR SEARCHES FOR SURVIVORS

HEROIC POLICE DOG OF 9/11

BY **MATTHEW K. MANNING**   ILLUSTRATED BY **MARK SIMMONS**

CAPSTONE PRESS
a capstone imprint

Published by Capstone Press, an imprint of Capstone.
1710 Roe Crest Drive, North Mankato, Minnesota 56003
capstonepub.com

Library of Congress Cataloging-in-Publication Data
is available on the Library of Congress website.

ISBN: 9781669057741 (hardcover)
ISBN: 9781669057963 (paperback)
ISBN: 9781669057970 (ebook PDF)

Summary:
On September 11, 2001, terrorists attacked the World Trade Center in New York City. Nearly 3,000 people were killed, and many were trapped under the collapsed buildings. When police officer James Symington heard about the attacks, he knew he and his German Shepherd, Trakr, had to help. Follow Trakr's lead as he and Symington bravely search and dig through the rubble to help rescue survivors of one of the deadliest days in U.S. history.

Editorial Credits
Editor: Aaron Sautter; Designer: Elyse White; Media Researcher: Rebekah Hubstenberger; Production Specialist: Whitney Schaefer

Image Credits
Associate Press: Stephen Chernin, 29

All internet sites appearing in back matter were available and accurate when this book was sent to press.

Direct quotes appear in **bold, *italicized*** text on the following pages:

Pages 13, 21, 22: from Woestendiek, John. *Dog, Inc.: The Uncanny Inside Story of Cloning Man's Best Friend*. New York: Avery, 2010.

Pages 22–23: from "9/11: The Last Person Pulled Out Alive from World Trade Center Rubble: 'I Was Given a New Life,'" by Diane Herbst, *People Magazine*, 2021.

TABLE OF CONTENTS

Chapter 1: Born and Bred 4

Chapter 2: A Nose for Danger 8

Chapter 3: In Search of Hope 14

Chapter 4: The Final Rescue 18

Chapter 5: A New Leash on Life 26

Trakr Tales 29
Glossary 30
Read More 31
Internet Sites 31
About the Author 32
About the Illustrator 32

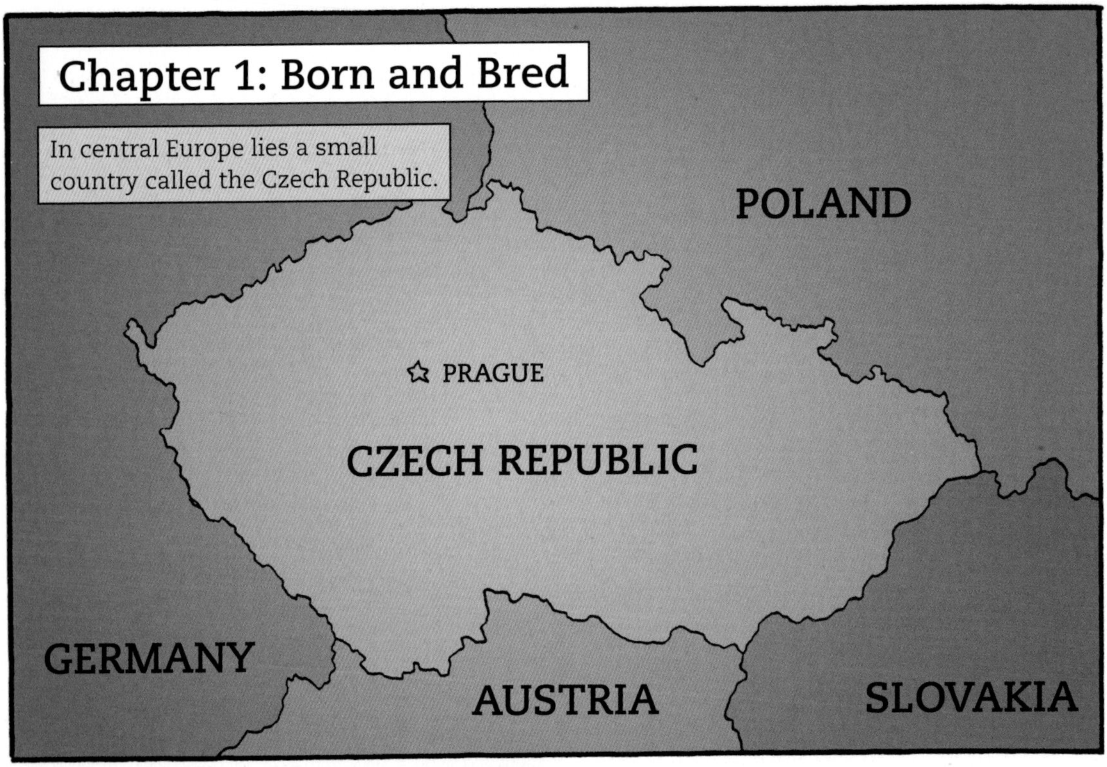
Chapter 1: Born and Bred
In central Europe lies a small country called the Czech Republic.
POLAND
PRAGUE
CZECH REPUBLIC
GERMANY
AUSTRIA
SLOVAKIA

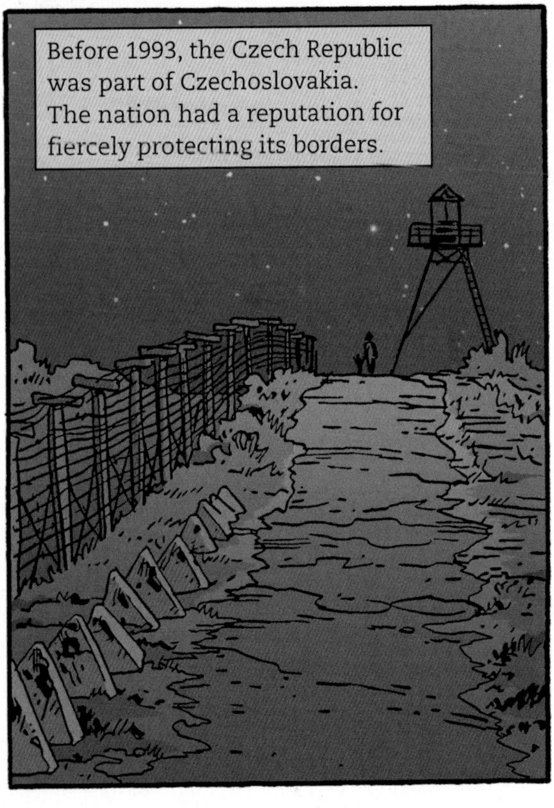
Before 1993, the Czech Republic was part of Czechoslovakia. The nation had a reputation for fiercely protecting its borders.

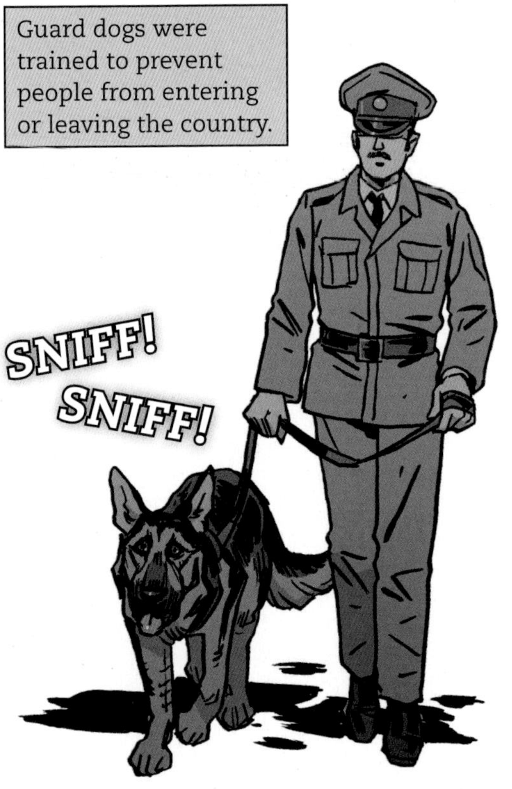
Guard dogs were trained to prevent people from entering or leaving the country.
SNIFF!
SNIFF!

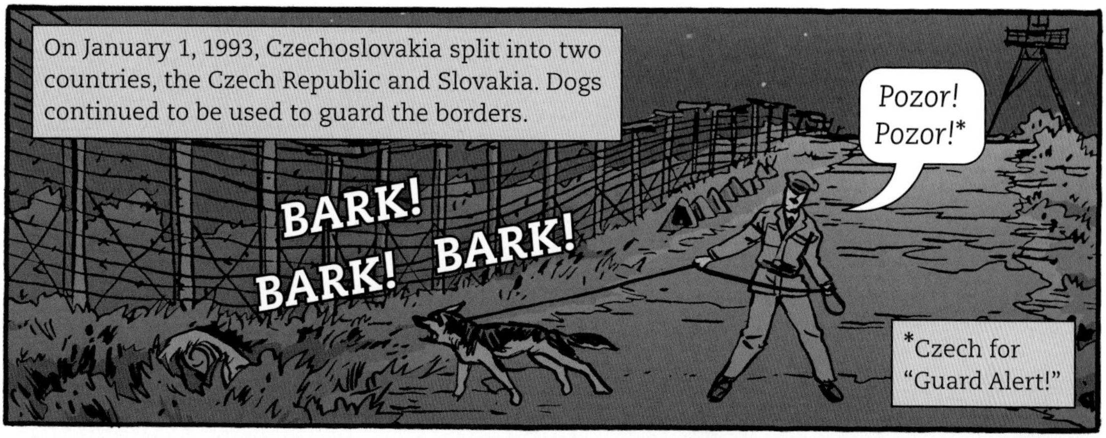
On January 1, 1993, Czechoslovakia split into two countries, the Czech Republic and Slovakia. Dogs continued to be used to guard the borders.
Pozor! Pozor!*
BARK!
BARK! BARK!
*Czech for "Guard Alert!"

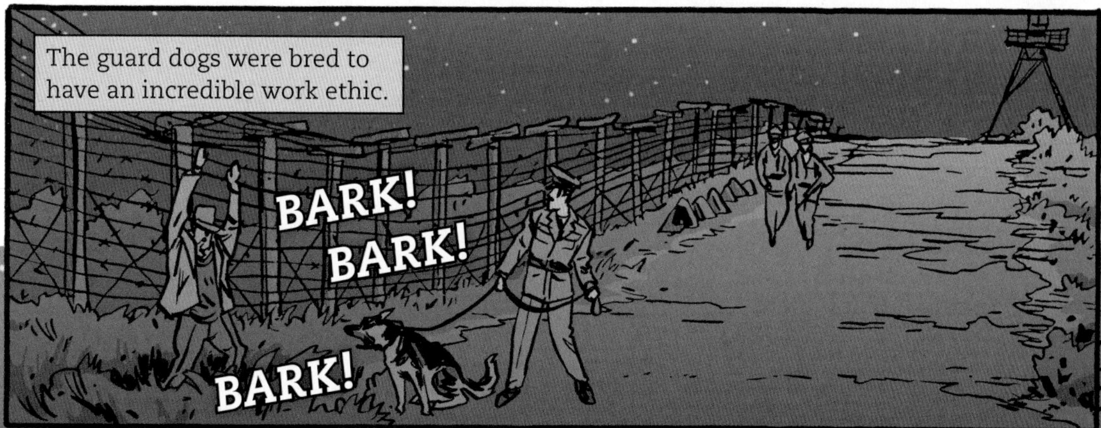
The guard dogs were bred to have an incredible work ethic.
BARK!
BARK!
BARK!

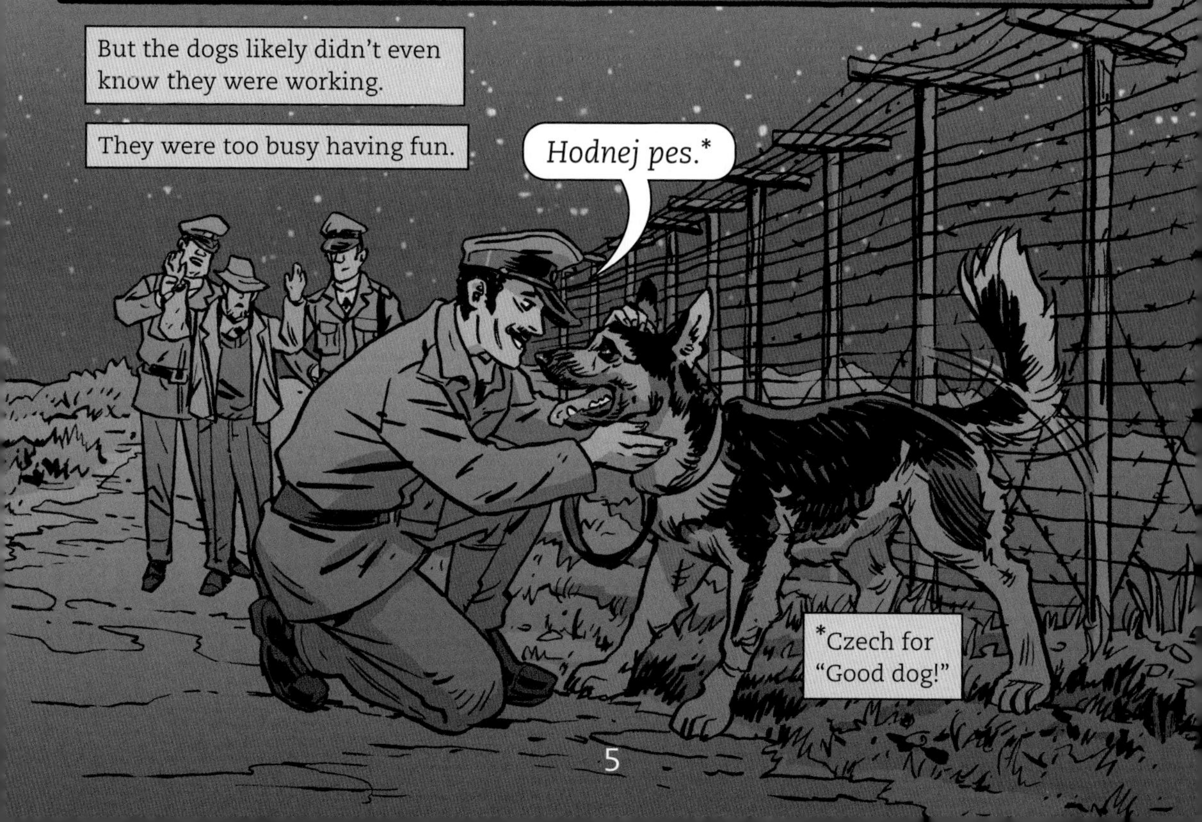
But the dogs likely didn't even know they were working.
They were too busy having fun.
*Hodnej pes.**
*Czech for "Good dog!"

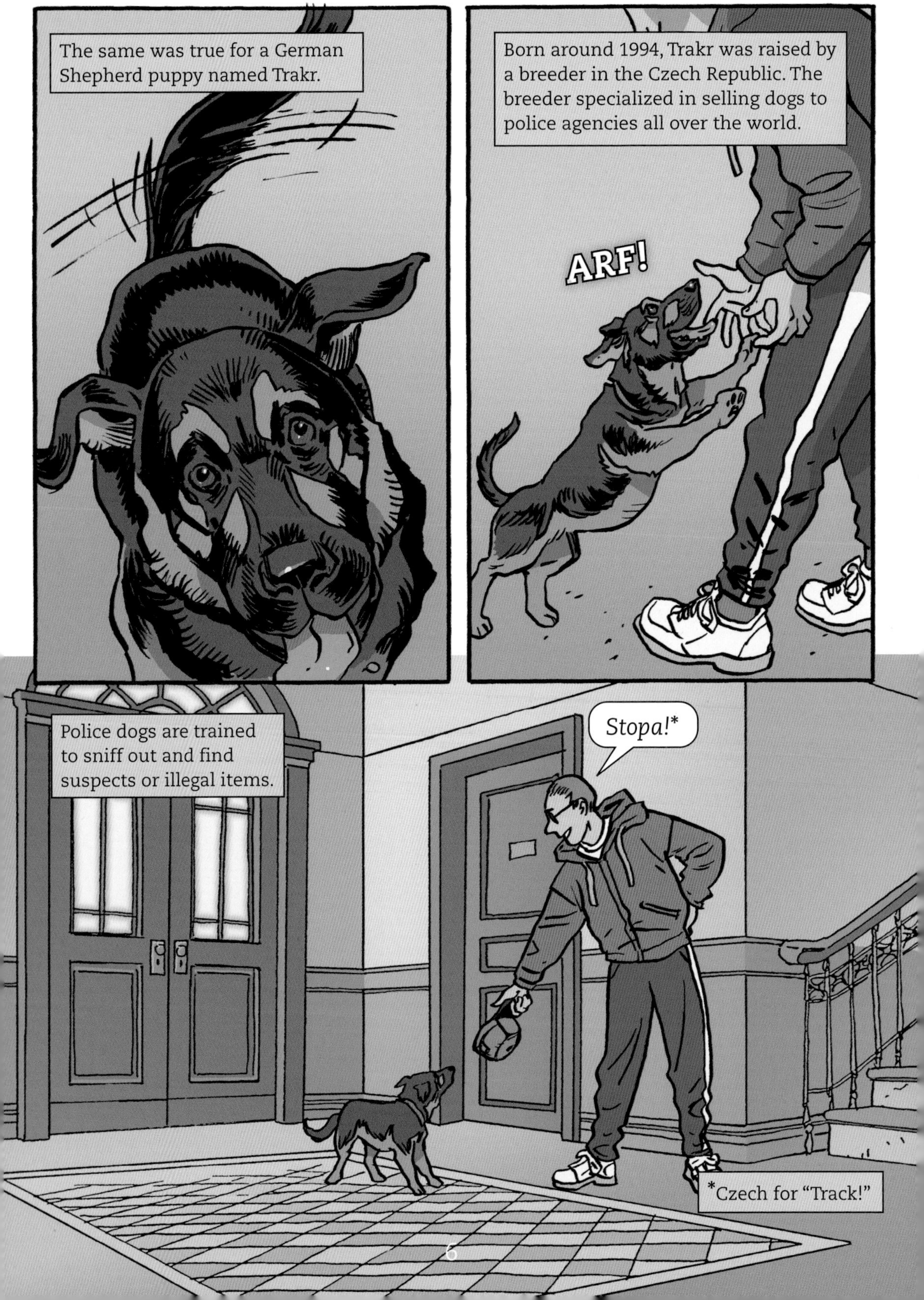
The same was true for a German Shepherd puppy named Trakr.
Born around 1994, Trakr was raised by a breeder in the Czech Republic. The breeder specialized in selling dogs to police agencies all over the world.
ARF!
Police dogs are trained to sniff out and find suspects or illegal items.
*Stopa!**
*Czech for "Track!"

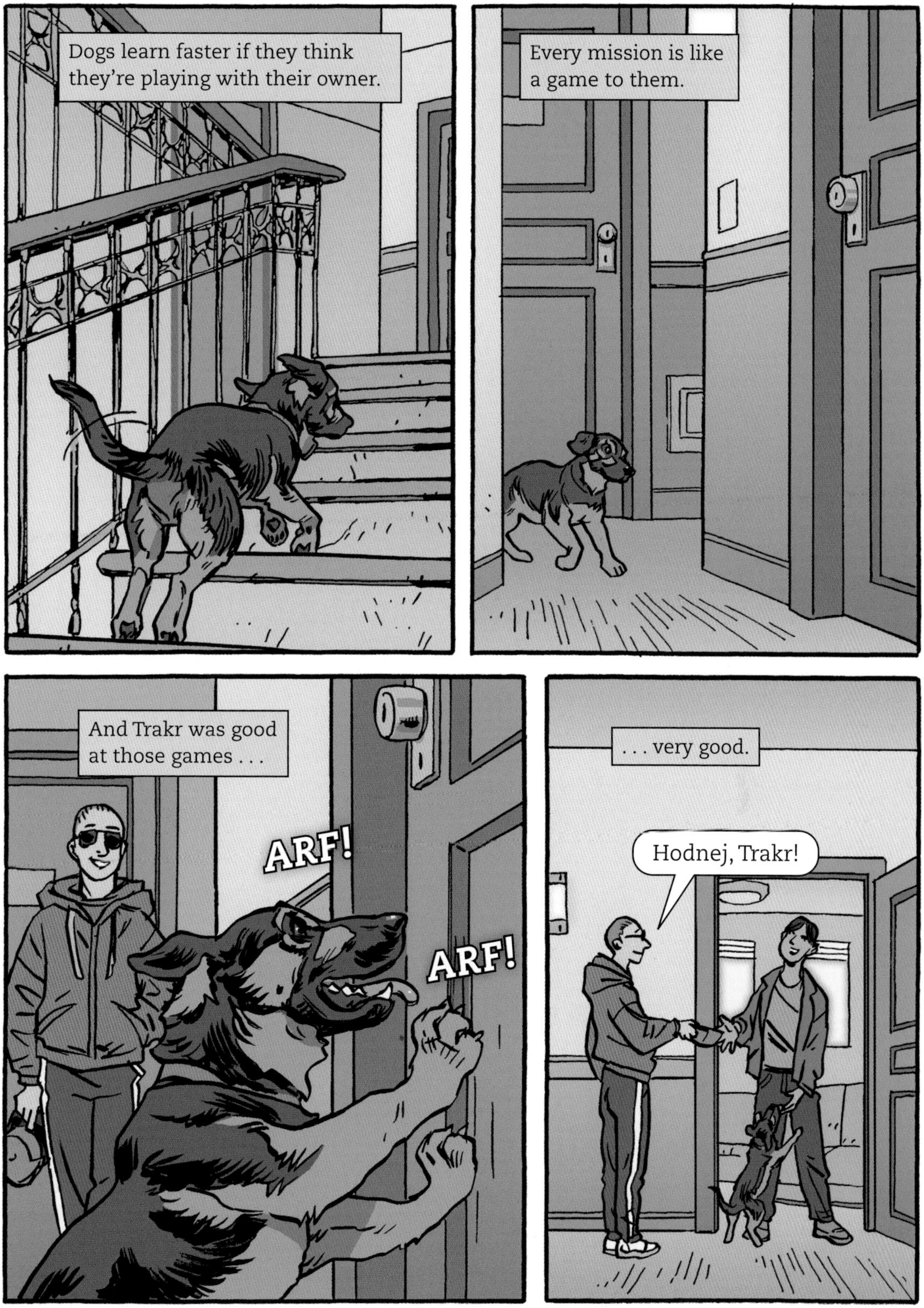
Dogs learn faster if they think they're playing with their owner.
Every mission is like a game to them.
And Trakr was good at those games . . .
ARF!
ARF!
. . . very good.
Hodnej, Trakr!

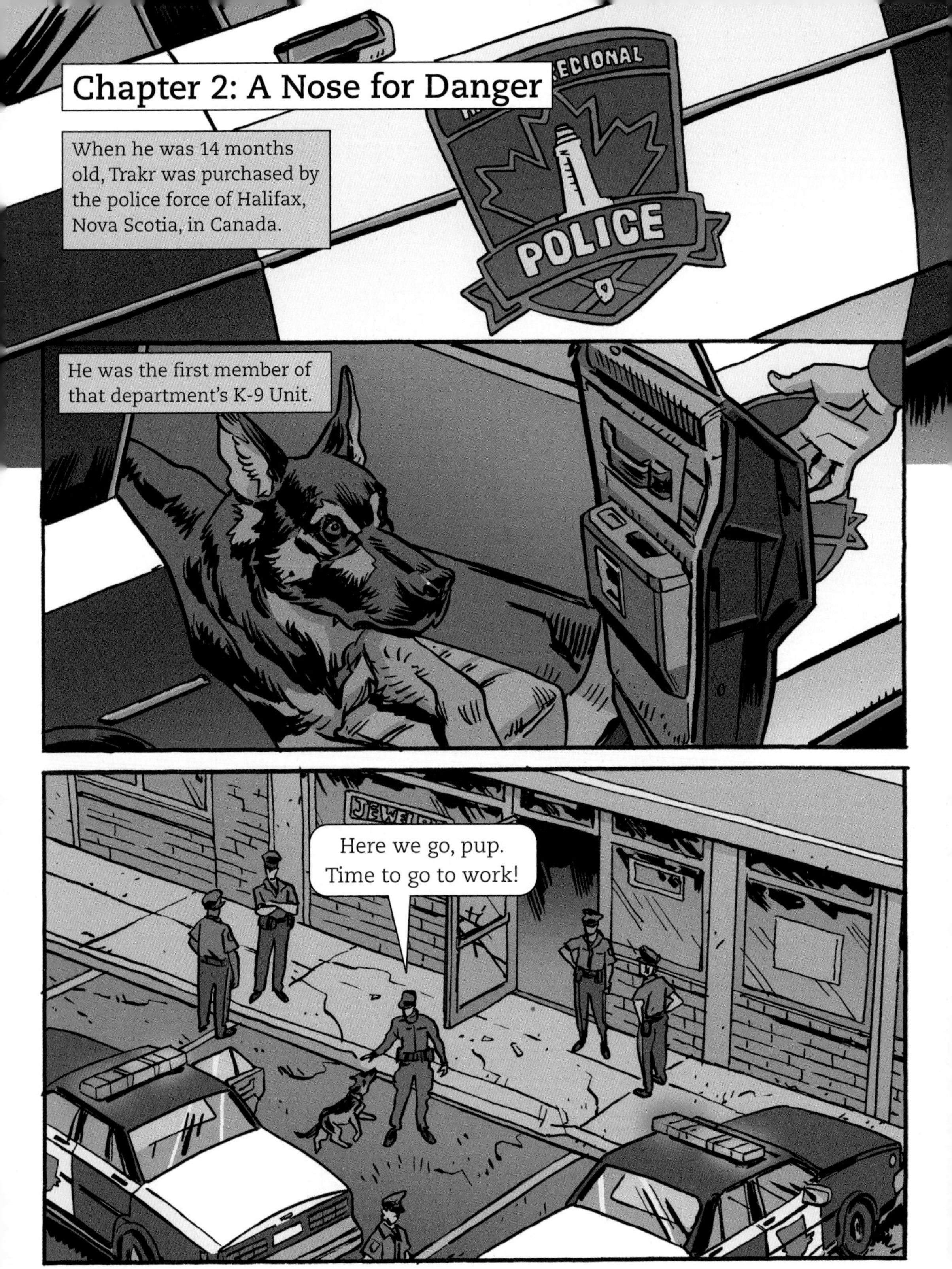
Chapter 2: A Nose for Danger
When he was 14 months old, Trakr was purchased by the police force of Halifax, Nova Scotia, in Canada.
POLICE
He was the first member of that department's K-9 Unit.
Here we go, pup. Time to go to work!

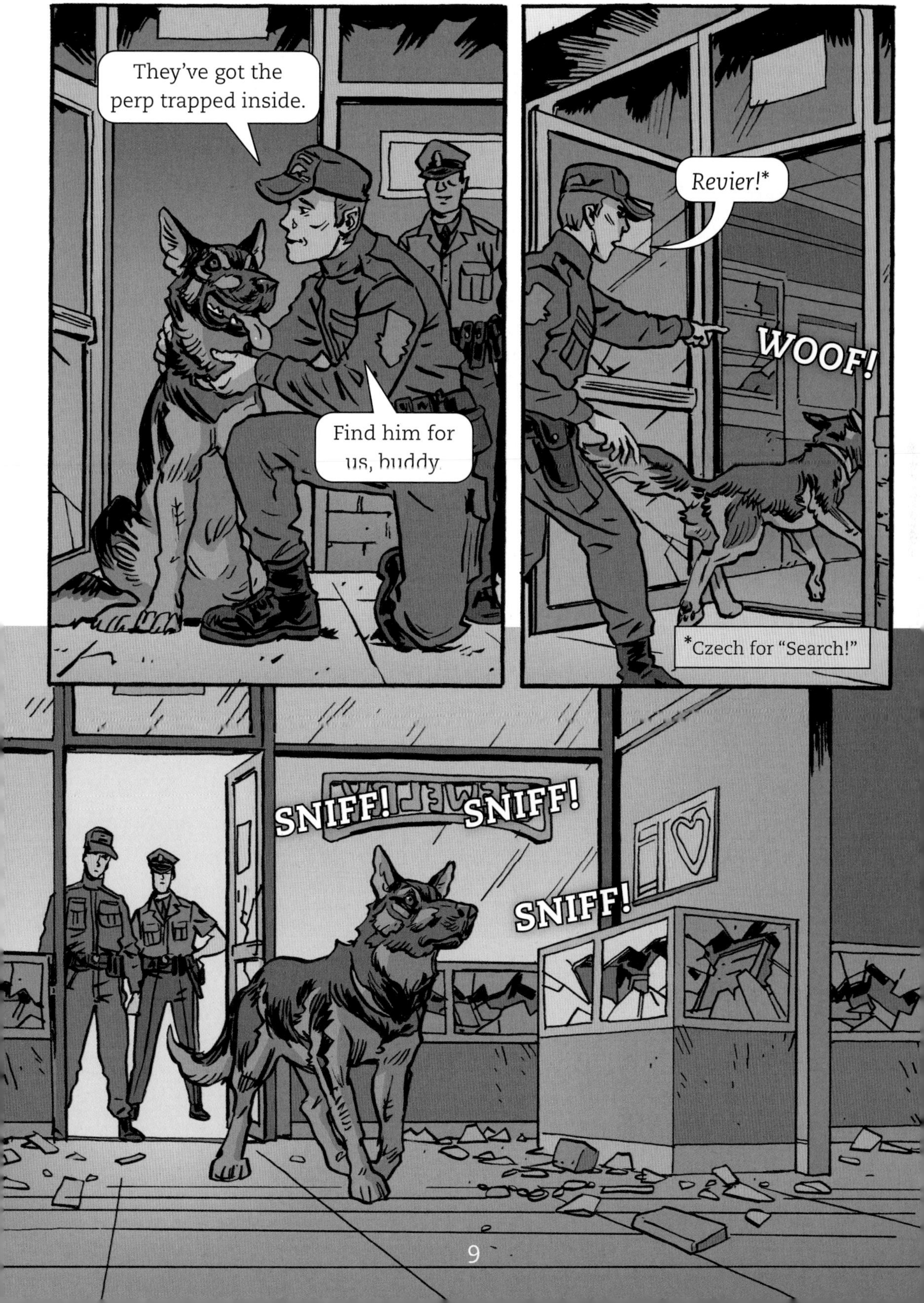
They've got the perp trapped inside.
Find him for us, buddy.
Revier!*
WOOF!
*Czech for "Search!"
SNIFF! SNIFF!
SNIFF!

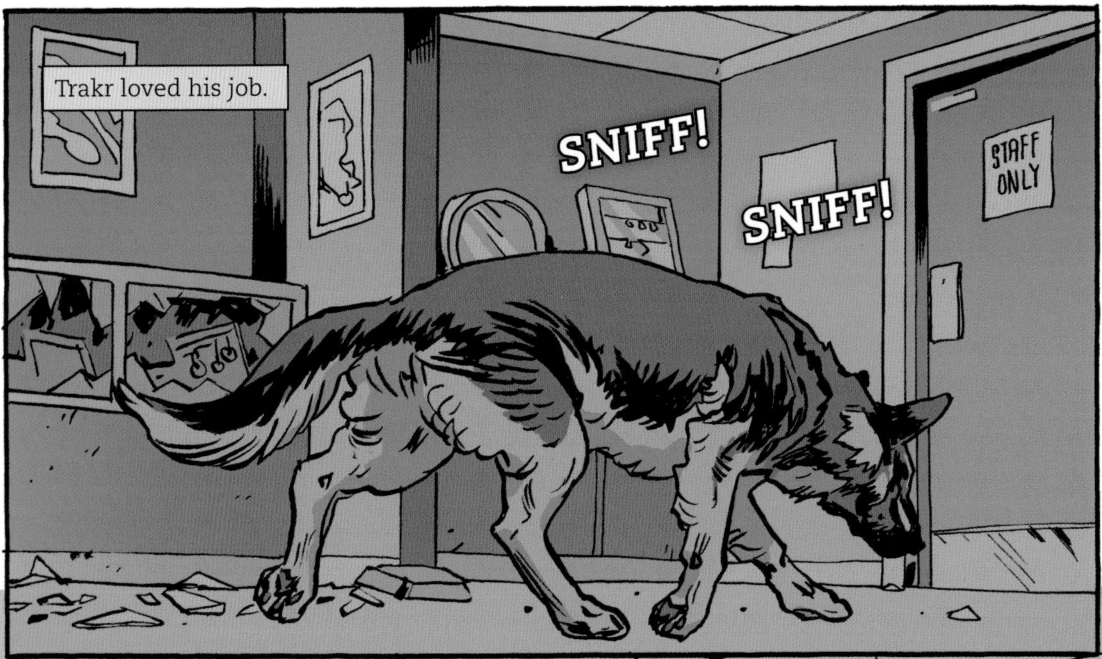
Trakr loved his job.
SNIFF!
SNIFF!
STAFF ONLY

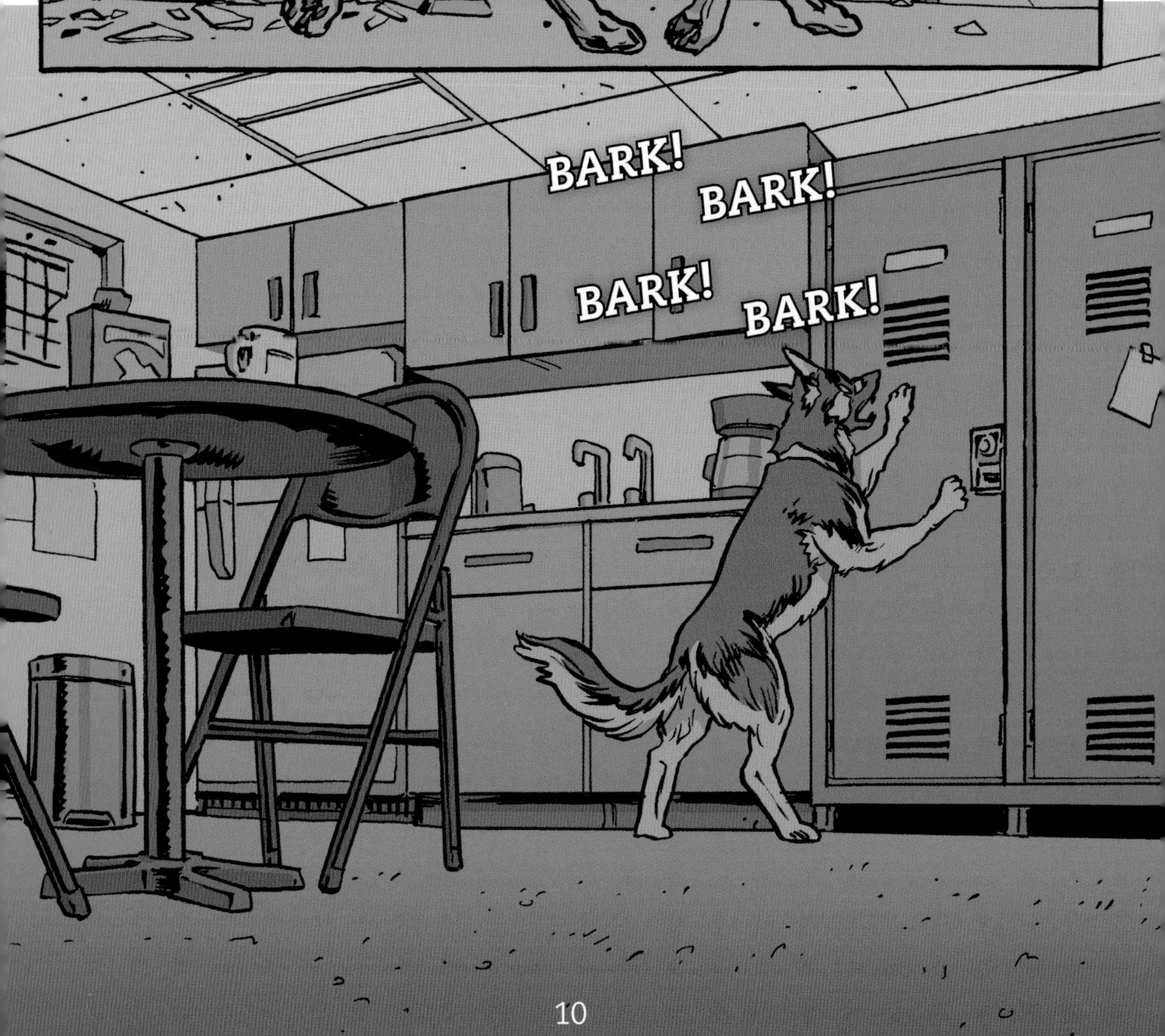
BARK!
BARK!
BARK!
BARK!

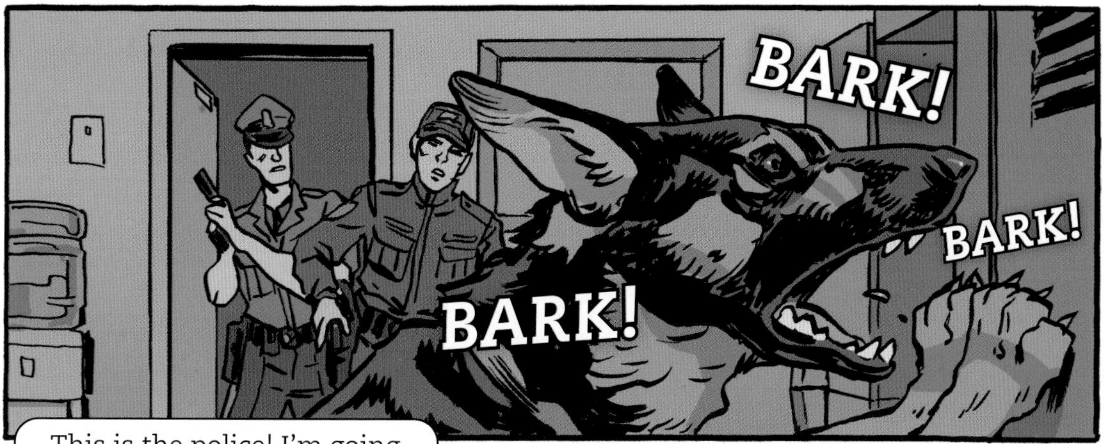
BARK!
BARK!
BARK!

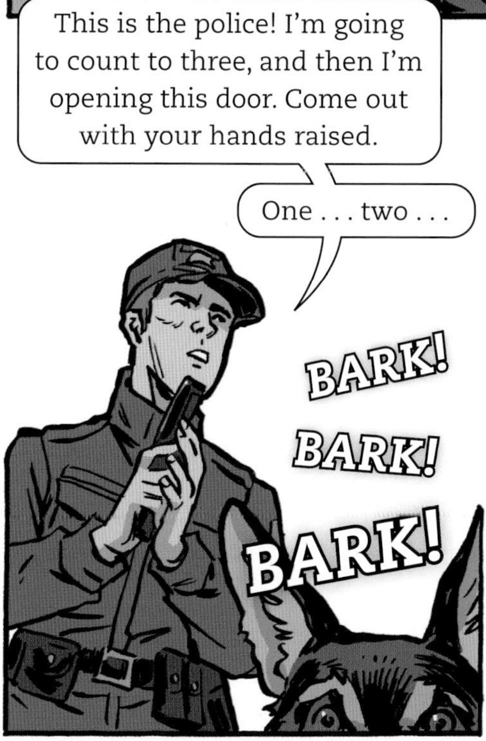
This is the police! I'm going to count to three, and then I'm opening this door. Come out with your hands raised.
One . . . two . . .
BARK!
BARK!
BARK!

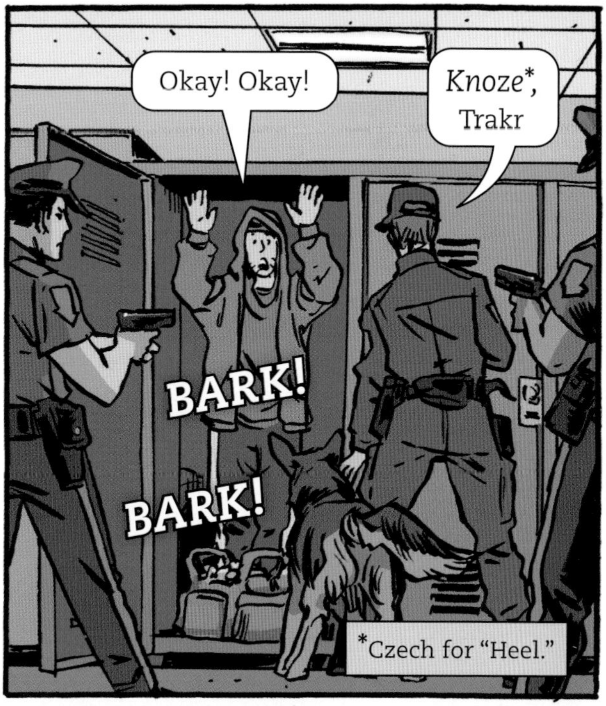
Okay! Okay!
*Knoze**, Trakr
BARK!
BARK!
*Czech for "Heel."

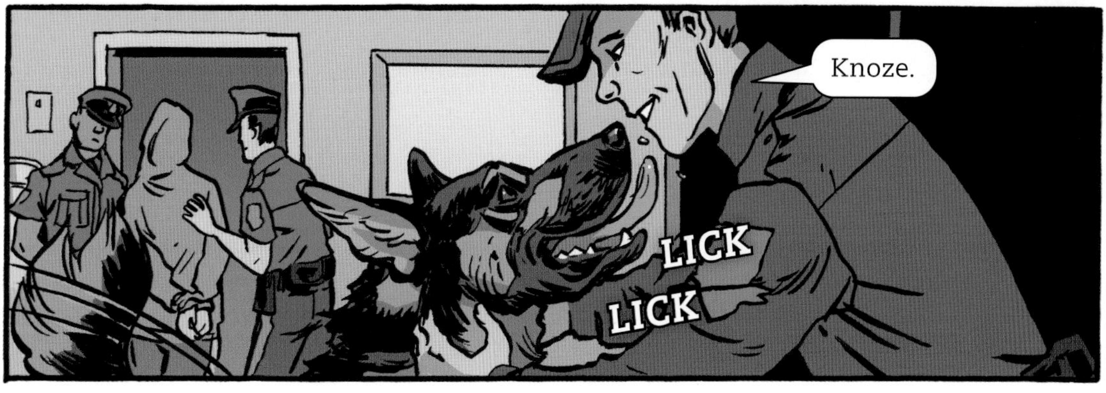
Knoze.
LICK
LICK

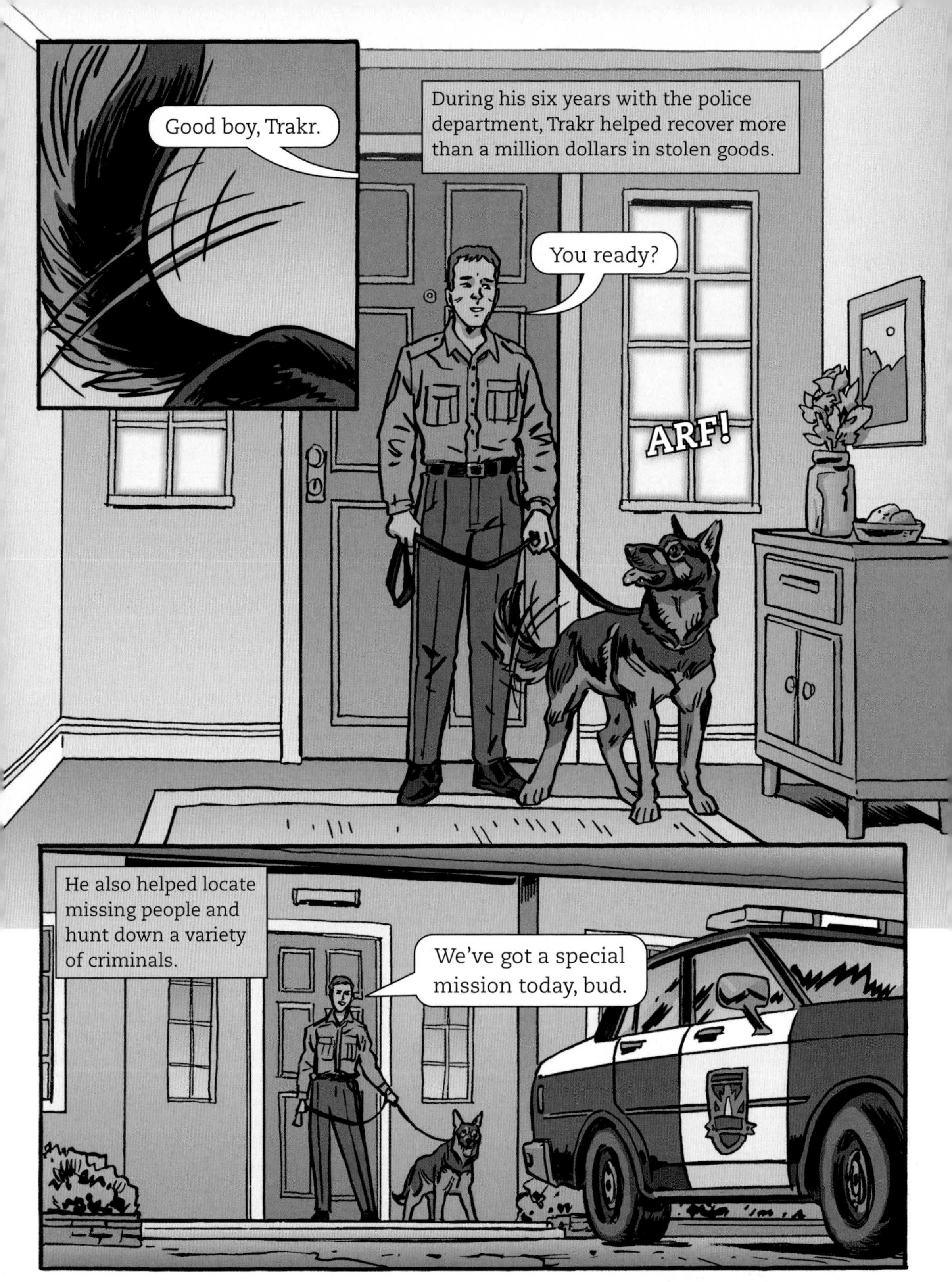
Good boy, Trakr.
During his six years with the police department, Trakr helped recover more than a million dollars in stolen goods.
You ready?
ARF!
He also helped locate missing people and hunt down a variety of criminals.
We've got a special mission today, bud.

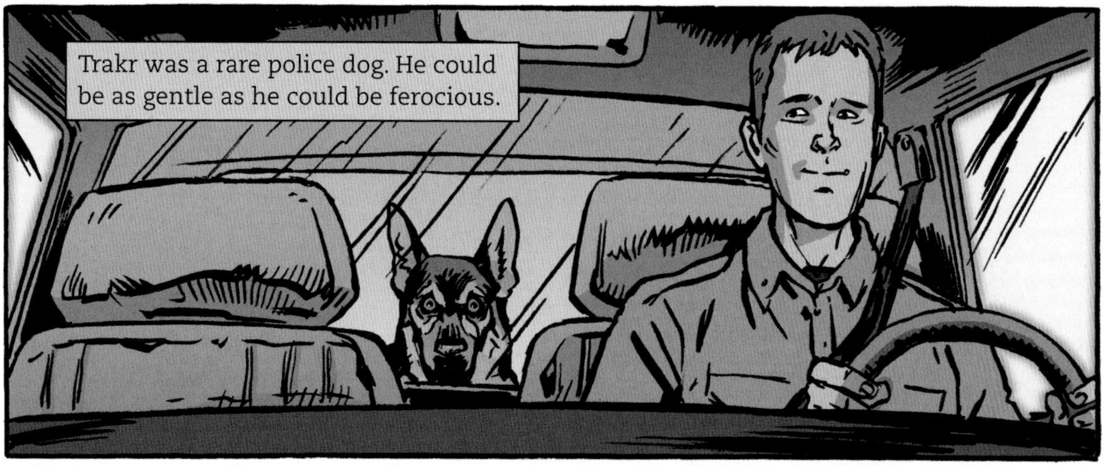
Trakr was a rare police dog. He could be as gentle as he could be ferocious.

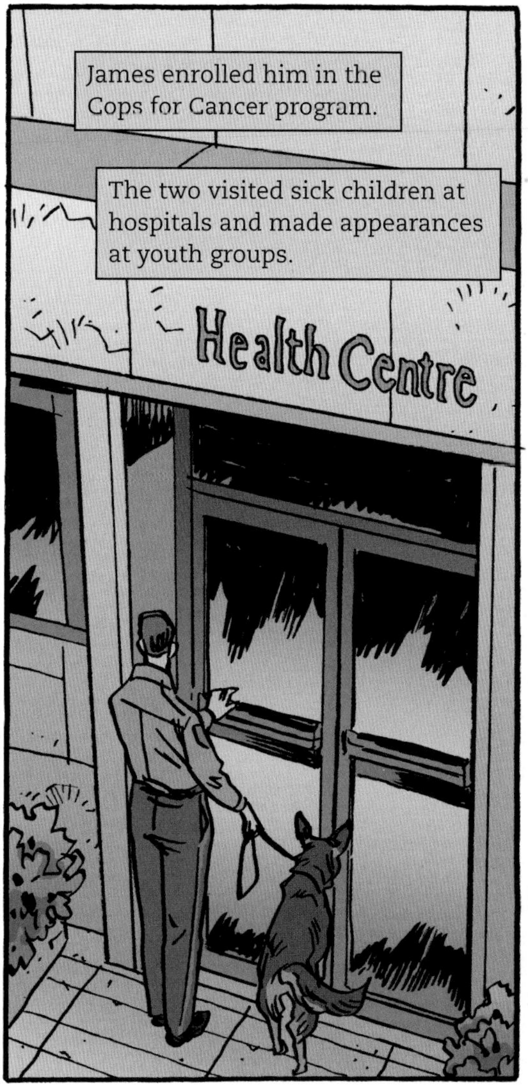
James enrolled him in the Cops for Cancer program.
The two visited sick children at hospitals and made appearances at youth groups.
Health Centre

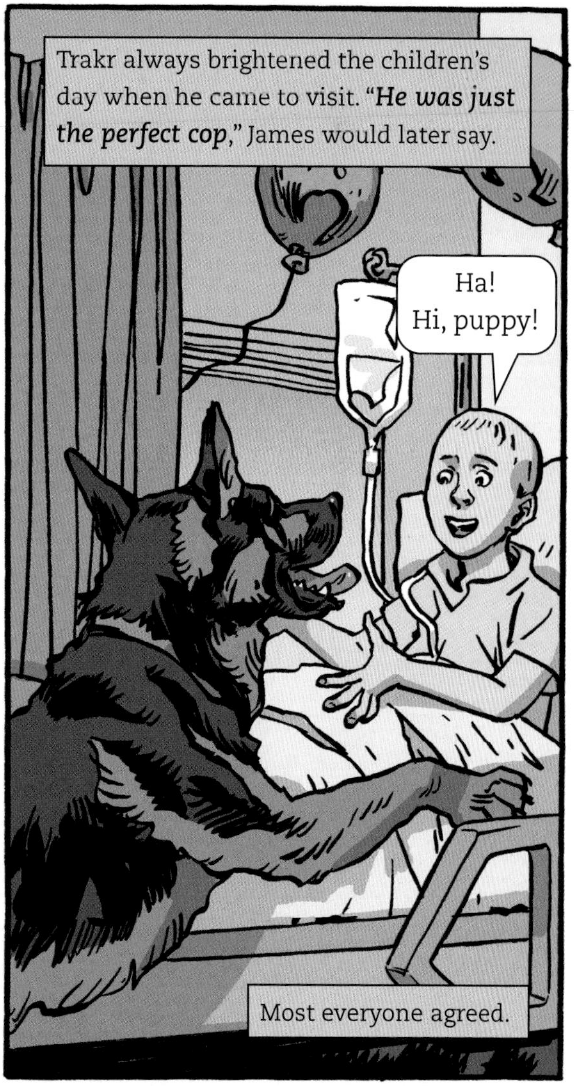
Trakr always brightened the children's day when he came to visit. "***He was just the perfect cop***," James would later say.
Ha! Hi, puppy!
Most everyone agreed.

Chapter 3: In Search of Hope

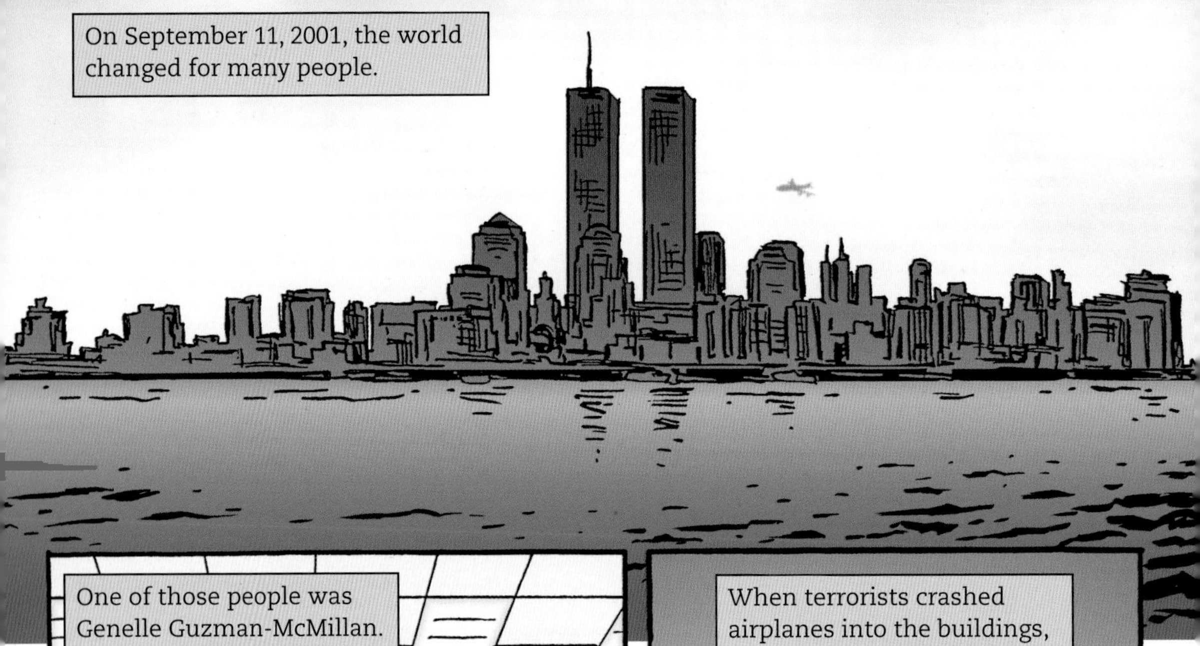
On September 11, 2001, the world changed for many people.

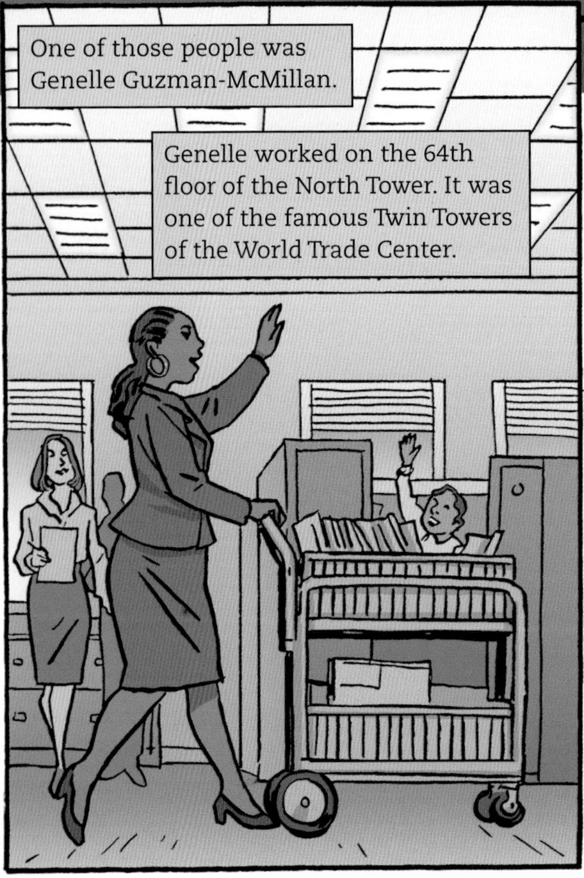
One of those people was Genelle Guzman-McMillan.
Genelle worked on the 64th floor of the North Tower. It was one of the famous Twin Towers of the World Trade Center.

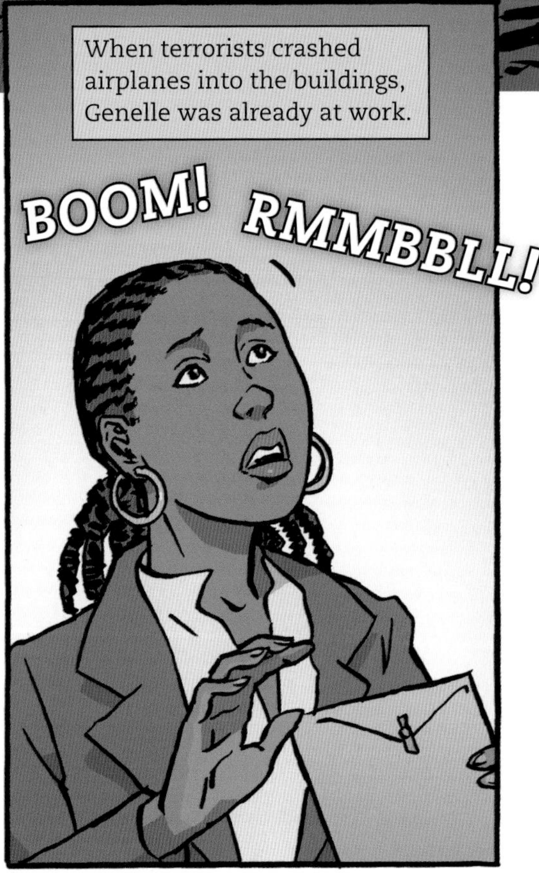
When terrorists crashed airplanes into the buildings, Genelle was already at work.
BOOM!
RMMBBLL!

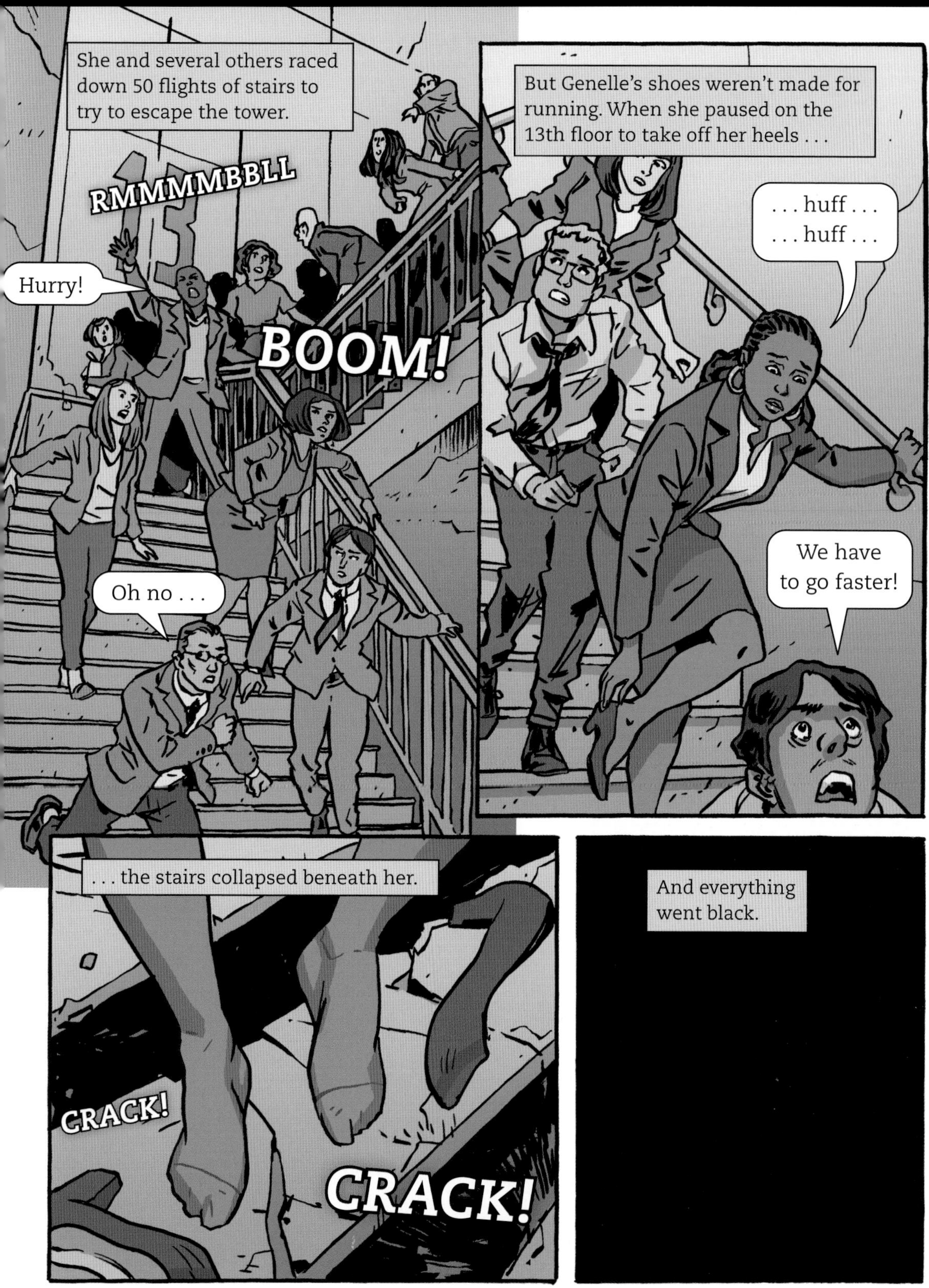
She and several others raced down 50 flights of stairs to try to escape the tower.
RMMMMMBBLL
Hurry!
BOOM!
Oh no . . .
But Genelle's shoes weren't made for running. When she paused on the 13th floor to take off her heels . . .
. . . huff . . .
. . . huff . . .
We have to go faster!
. . . the stairs collapsed beneath her.
CRACK!
CRACK!
And everything went black.

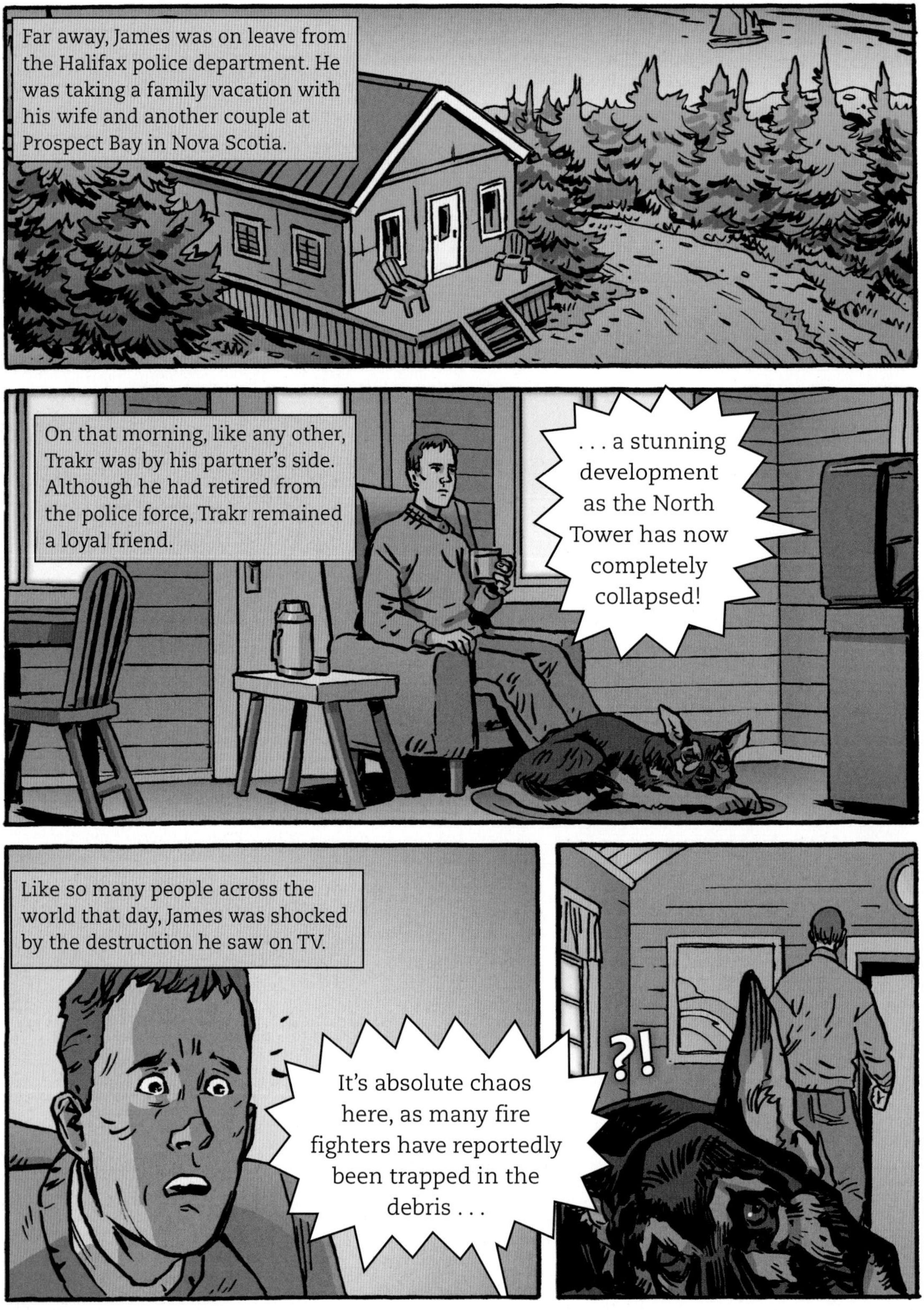
Far away, James was on leave from the Halifax police department. He was taking a family vacation with his wife and another couple at Prospect Bay in Nova Scotia.
On that morning, like any other, Trakr was by his partner's side. Although he had retired from the police force, Trakr remained a loyal friend.
. . . a stunning development as the North Tower has now completely collapsed!
Like so many people across the world that day, James was shocked by the destruction he saw on TV.
It's absolute chaos here, as many fire fighters have reportedly been trapped in the debris . . .
?!

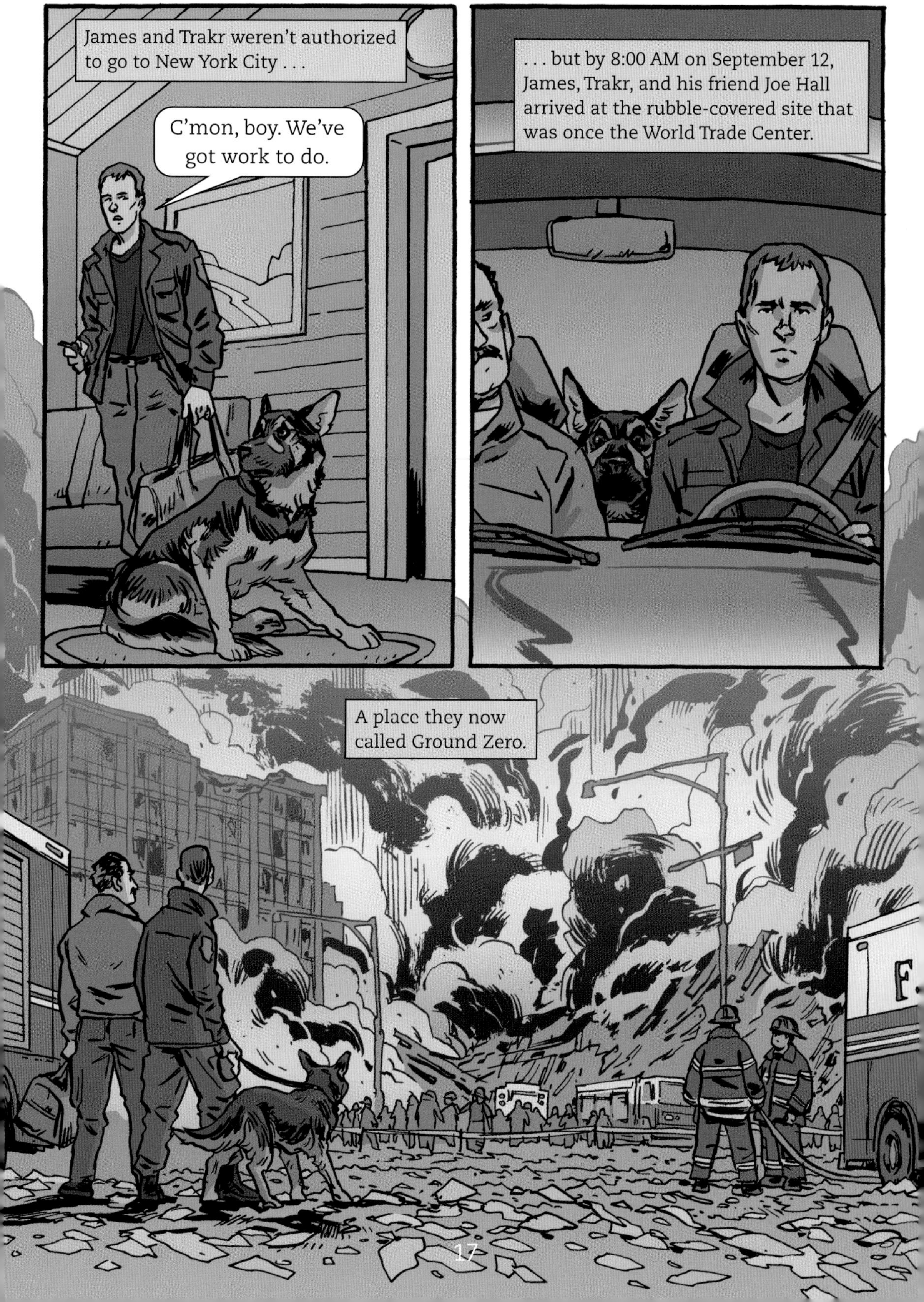
James and Trakr weren't authorized to go to New York City . . .
C'mon, boy. We've got work to do.
. . . but by 8:00 AM on September 12, James, Trakr, and his friend Joe Hall arrived at the rubble-covered site that was once the World Trade Center.
A place they now called Ground Zero.
F

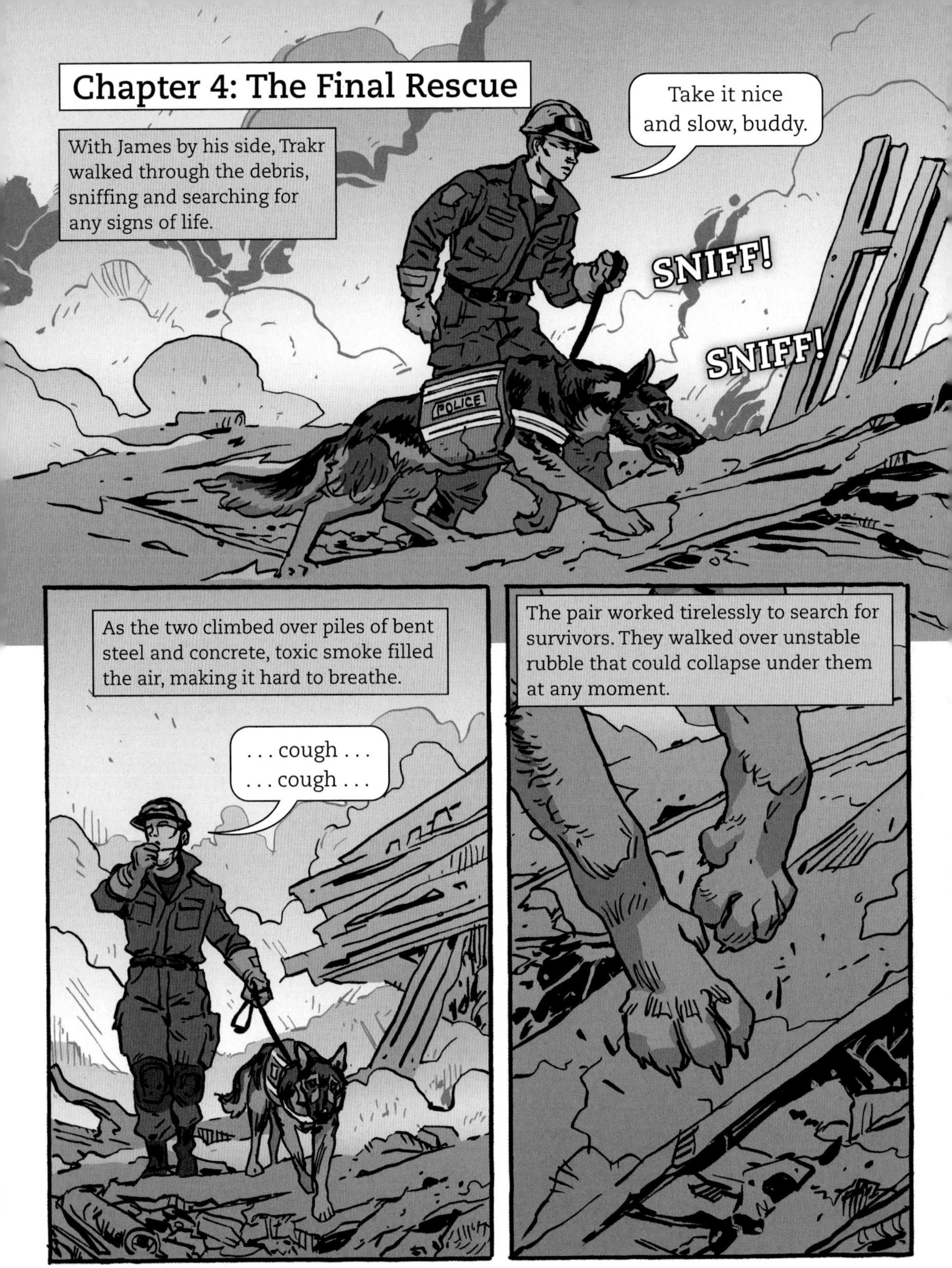
Chapter 4: The Final Rescue
With James by his side, Trakr walked through the debris, sniffing and searching for any signs of life.
Take it nice and slow, buddy.
SNIFF!
SNIFF!
POLICE
As the two climbed over piles of bent steel and concrete, toxic smoke filled the air, making it hard to breathe.
. . . cough . . .
. . . cough . . .
The pair worked tirelessly to search for survivors. They walked over unstable rubble that could collapse under them at any moment.

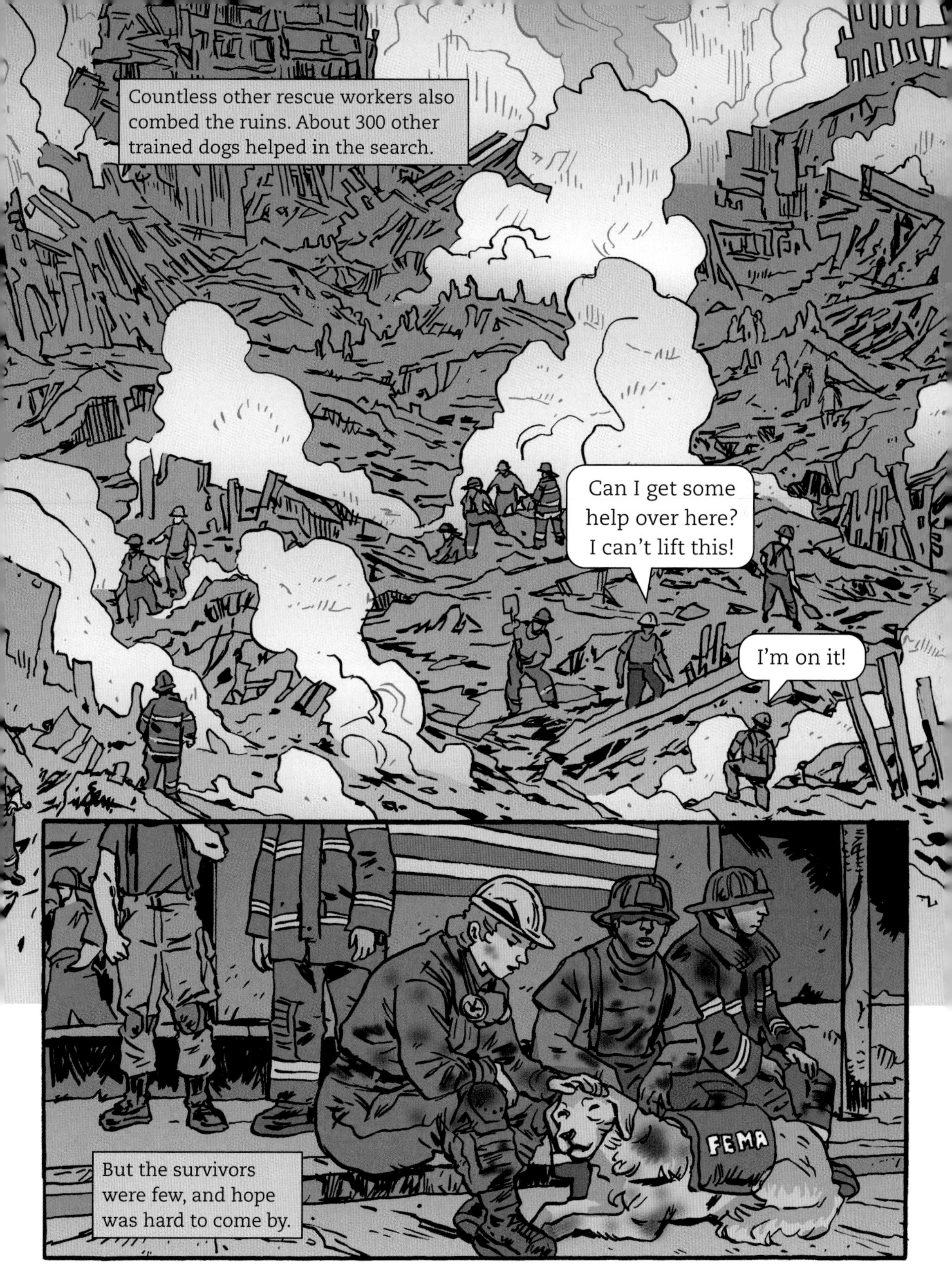
Countless other rescue workers also combed the ruins. About 300 other trained dogs helped in the search.
Can I get some help over here? I can't lift this!
I'm on it!
But the survivors were few, and hope was hard to come by.
FEMA

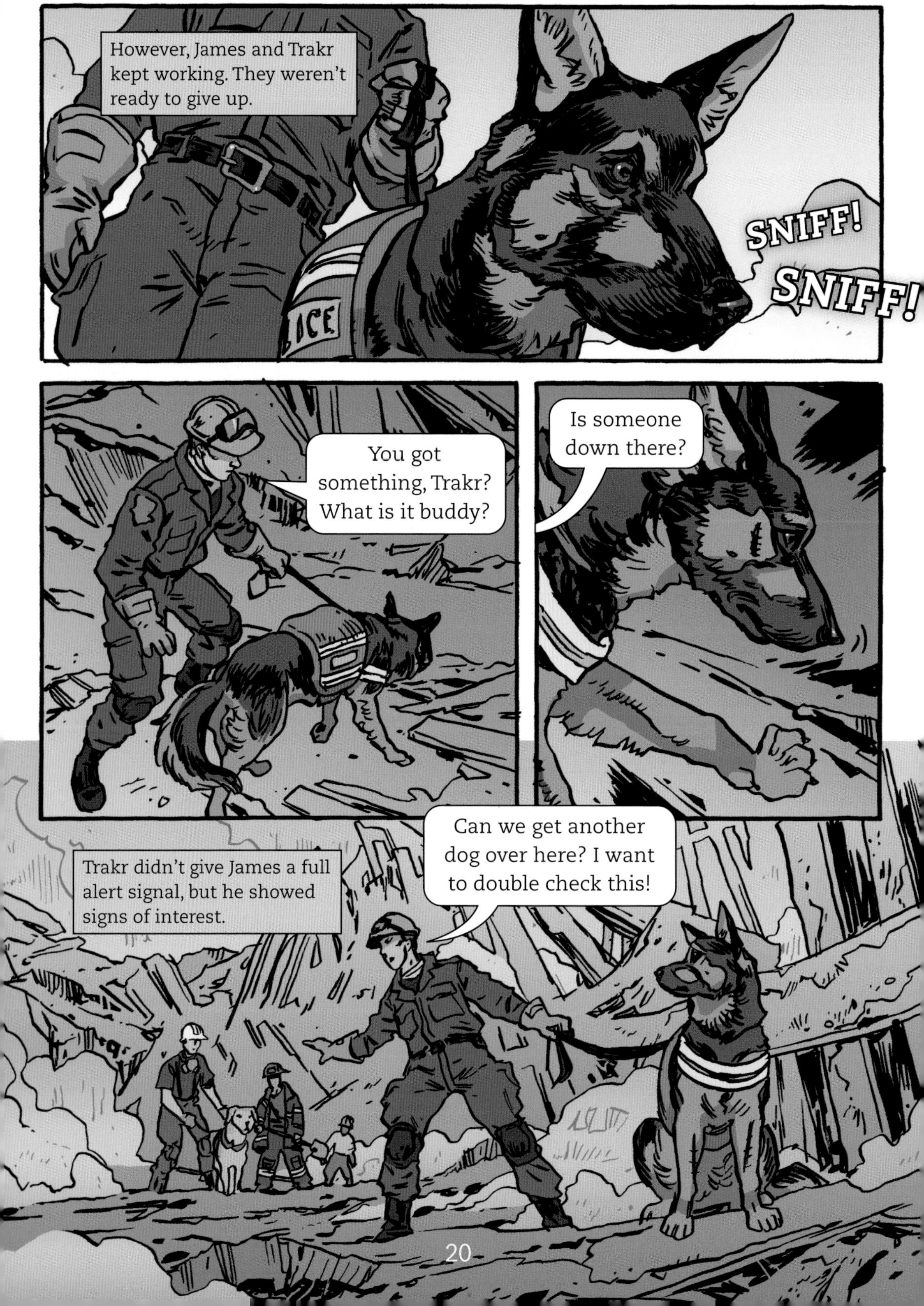
However, James and Trakr kept working. They weren't ready to give up.
SNIFF!
SNIFF!
ICE
You got something, Trakr? What is it buddy?
Is someone down there?
Trakr didn't give James a full alert signal, but he showed signs of interest.
Can we get another dog over here? I want to double check this!

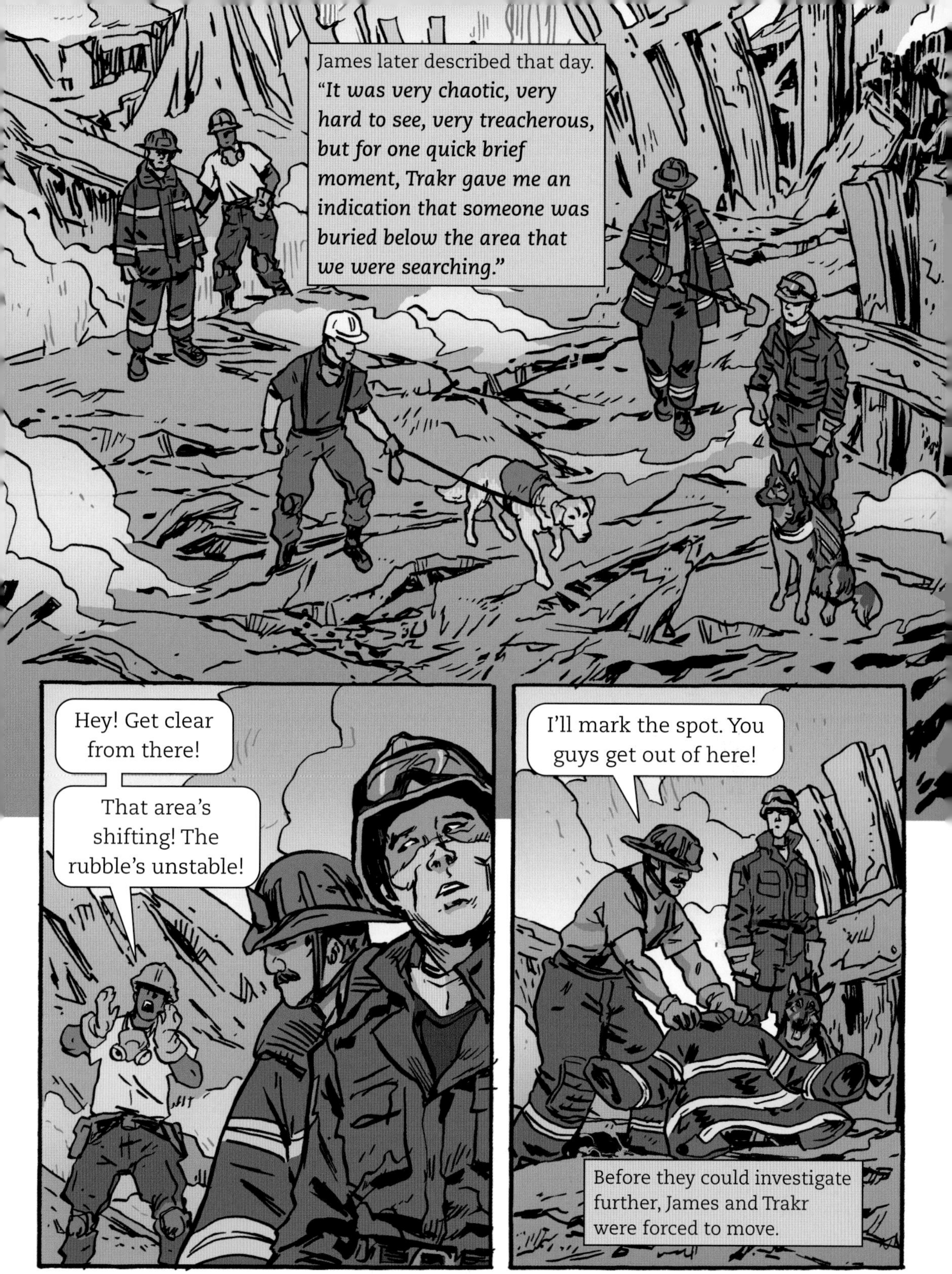
James later described that day. *"It was very chaotic, very hard to see, very treacherous, but for one quick brief moment, Trakr gave me an indication that someone was buried below the area that we were searching."*
Hey! Get clear from there!
That area's shifting! The rubble's unstable!
I'll mark the spot. You guys get out of here!
Before they could investigate further, James and Trakr were forced to move.

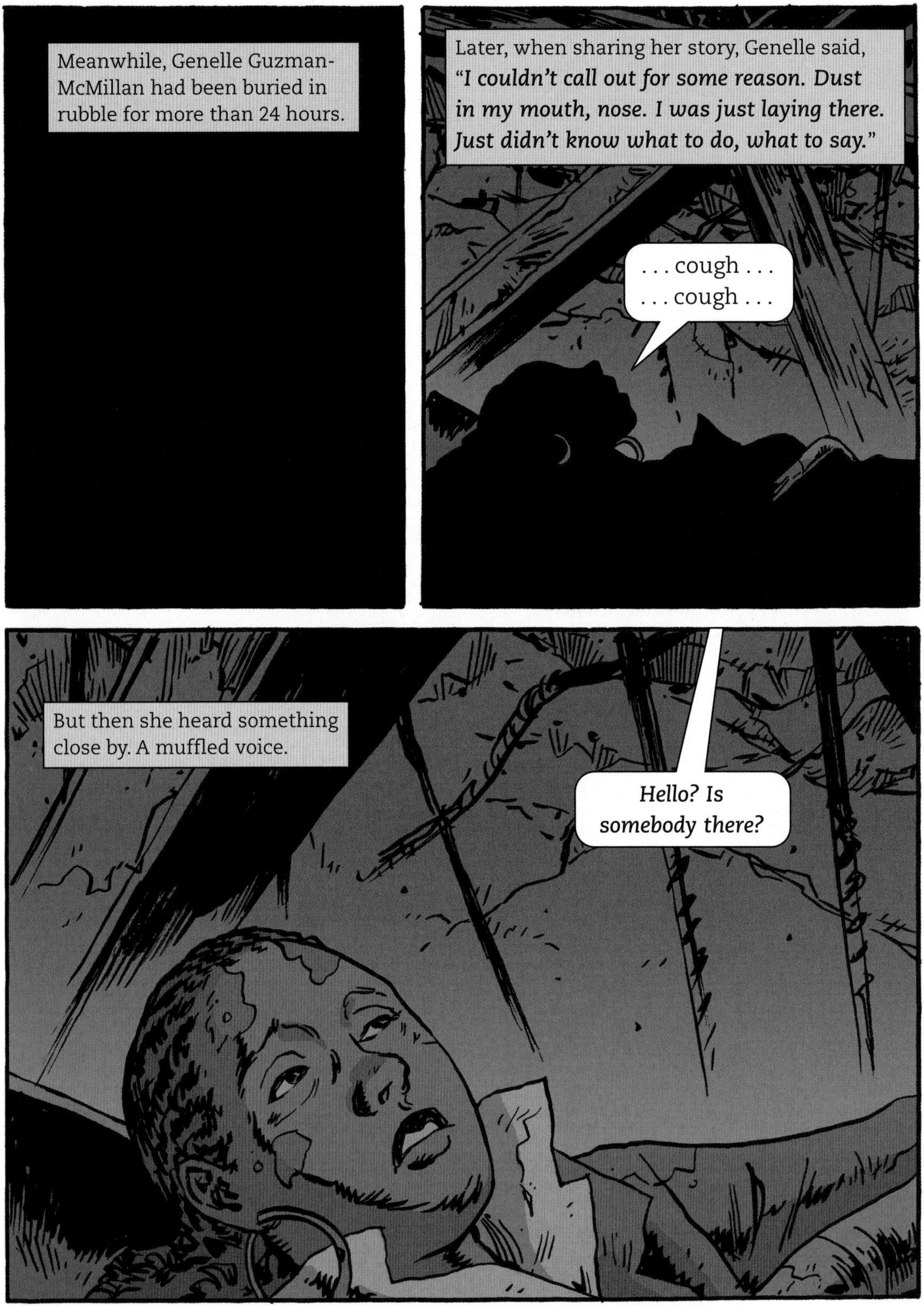
Meanwhile, Genelle Guzman-McMillan had been buried in rubble for more than 24 hours.
Later, when sharing her story, Genelle said, *"I couldn't call out for some reason. Dust in my mouth, nose. I was just laying there. Just didn't know what to do, what to say."*
. . . cough . . . . . . cough . . .
But then she heard something close by. A muffled voice.
Hello? Is somebody there?

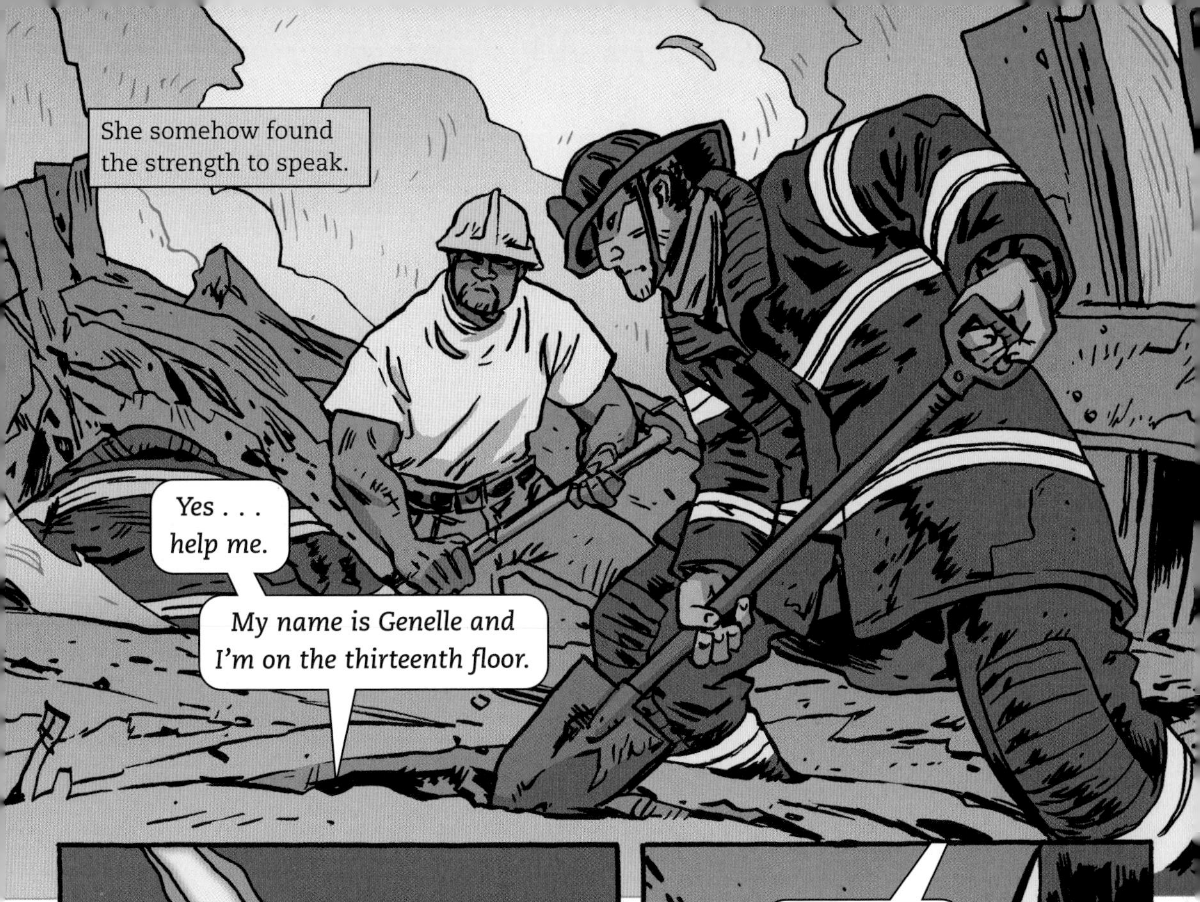
She somehow found the strength to speak.
Yes . . . help me.
My name is Genelle and I'm on the thirteenth floor.

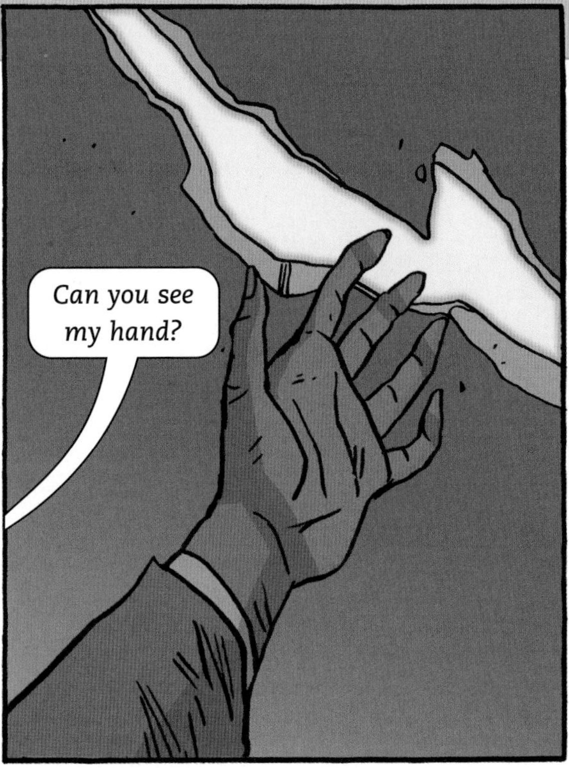
Can you see my hand?

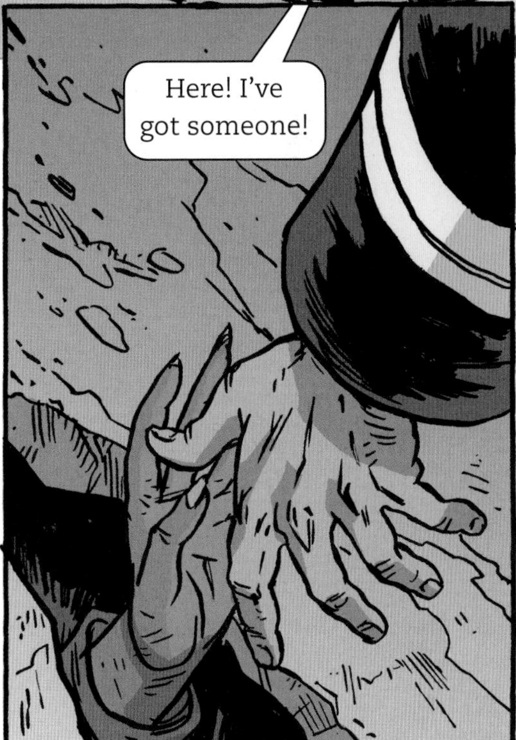
Here! I've got someone!

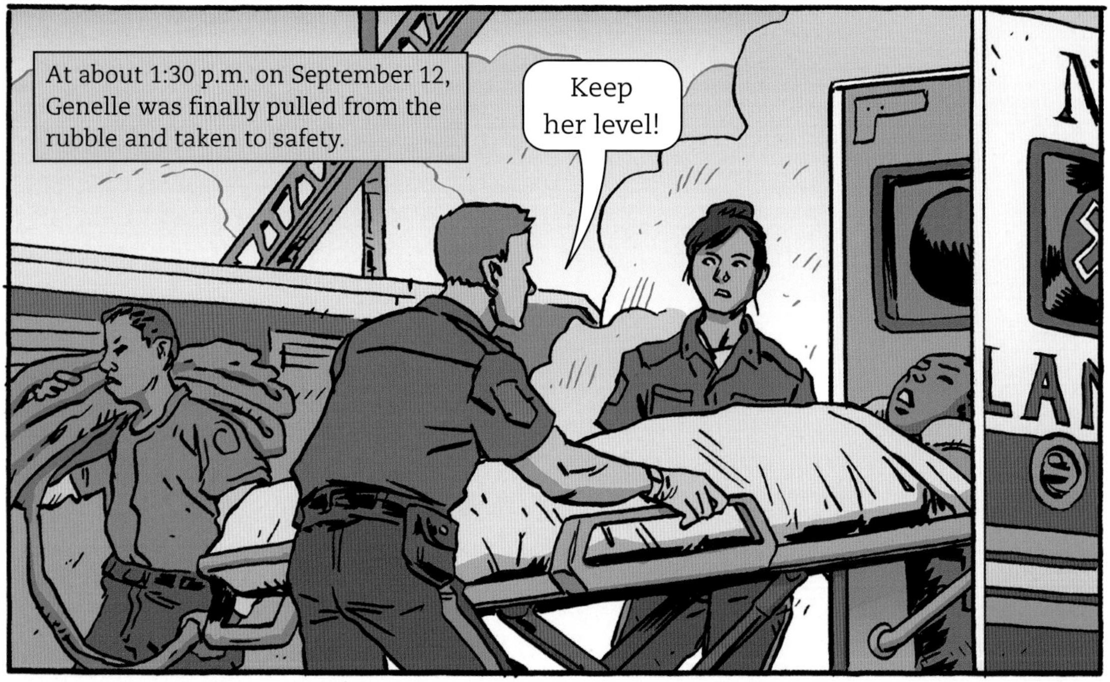
At about 1:30 p.m. on September 12, Genelle was finally pulled from the rubble and taken to safety.
Keep her level!

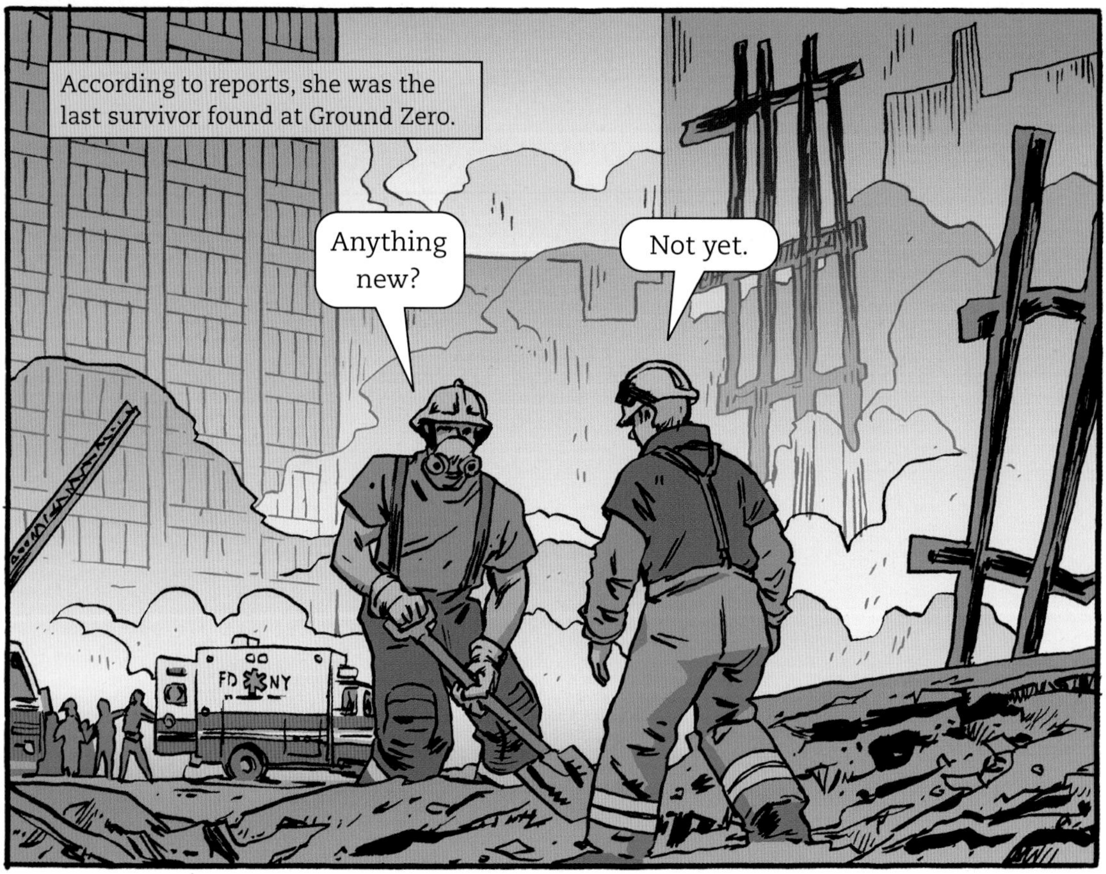
According to reports, she was the last survivor found at Ground Zero.
Anything new?
Not yet.
FDNY

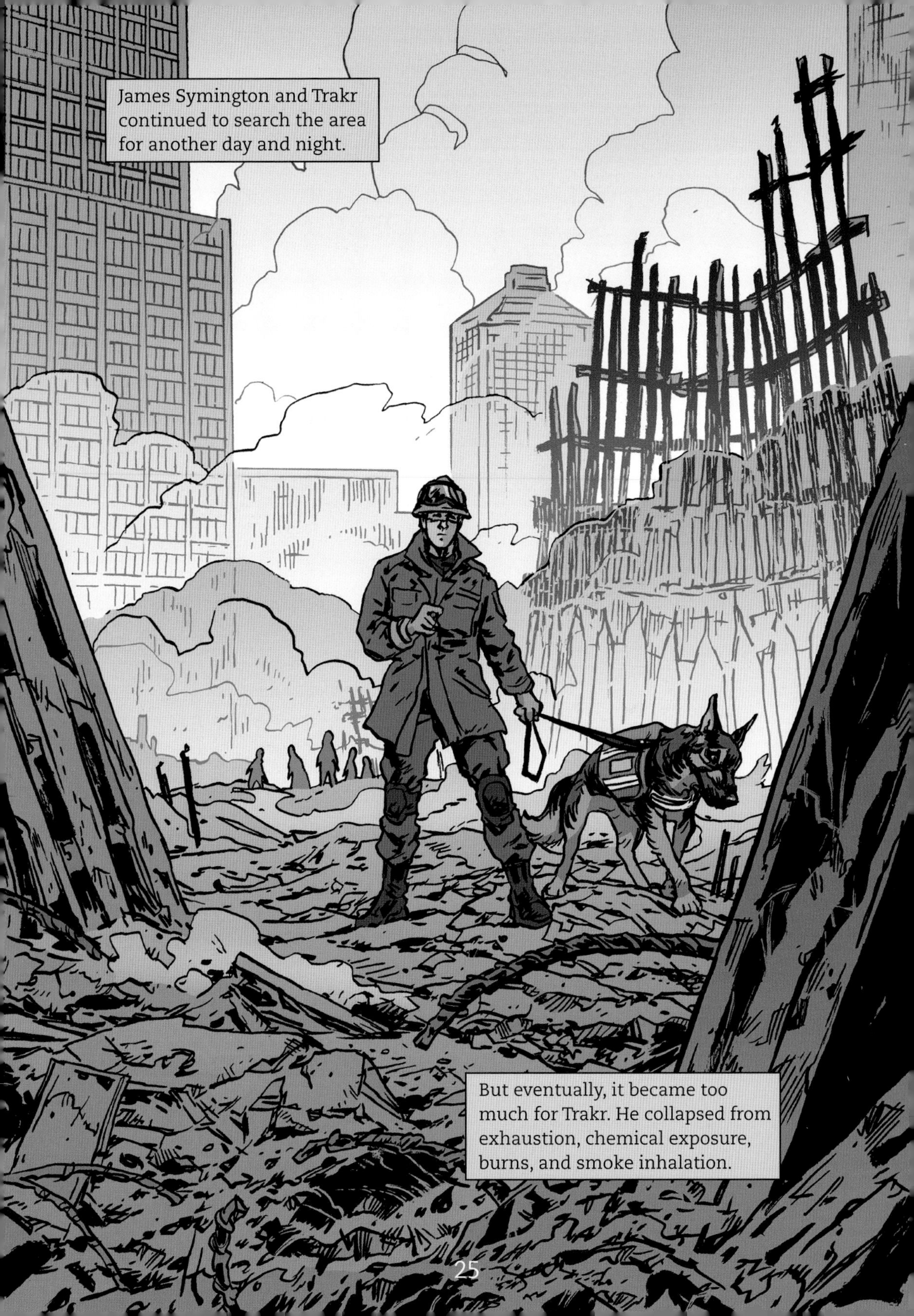
James Symington and Trakr continued to search the area for another day and night.
But eventually, it became too much for Trakr. He collapsed from exhaustion, chemical exposure, burns, and smoke inhalation.

Chapter 5: A New Leash on Life

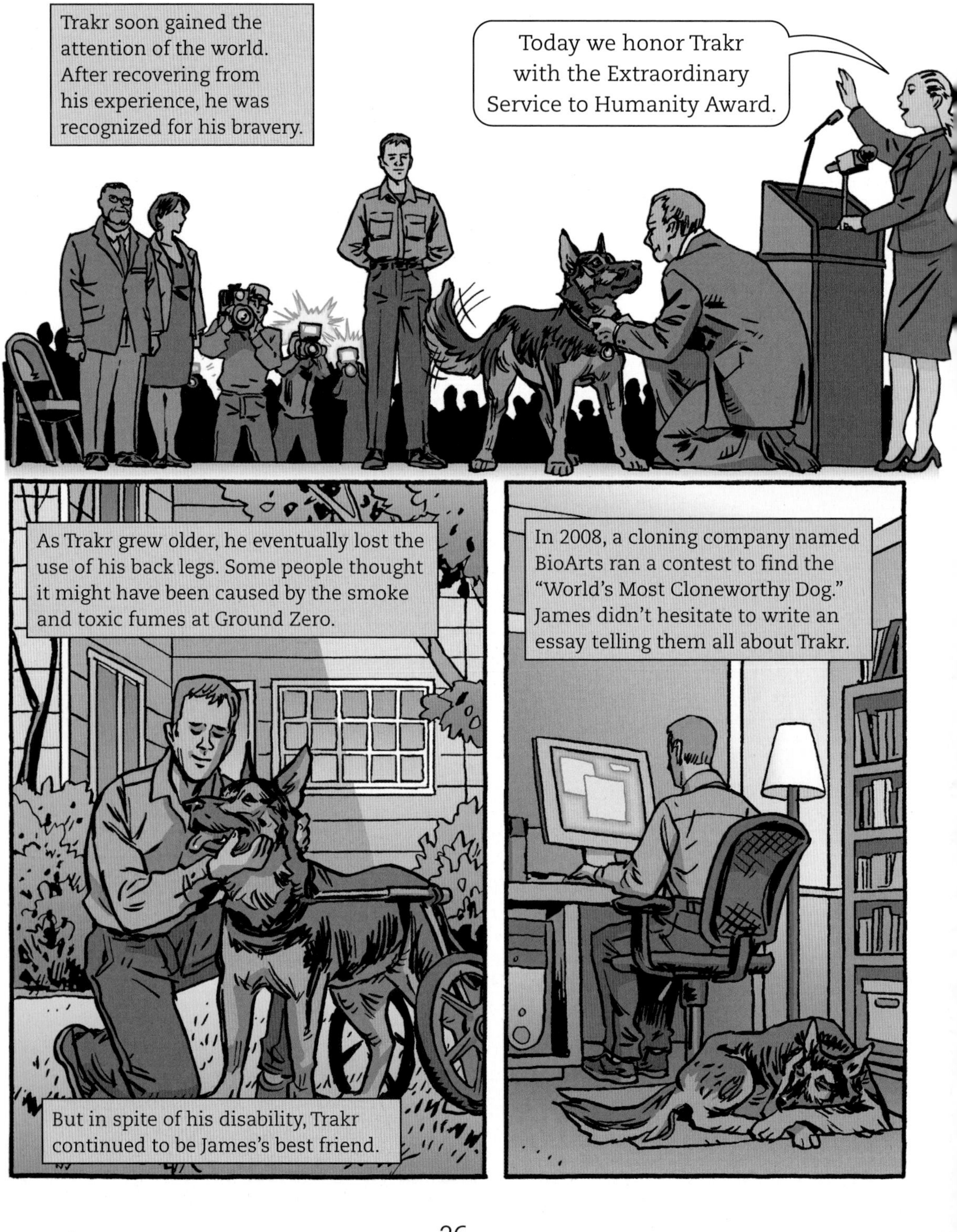
Trakr soon gained the attention of the world. After recovering from his experience, he was recognized for his bravery.
Today we honor Trakr with the Extraordinary Service to Humanity Award.
As Trakr grew older, he eventually lost the use of his back legs. Some people thought it might have been caused by the smoke and toxic fumes at Ground Zero.
But in spite of his disability, Trakr continued to be James's best friend.
In 2008, a cloning company named BioArts ran a contest to find the "World's Most Cloneworthy Dog." James didn't hesitate to write an essay telling them all about Trakr.

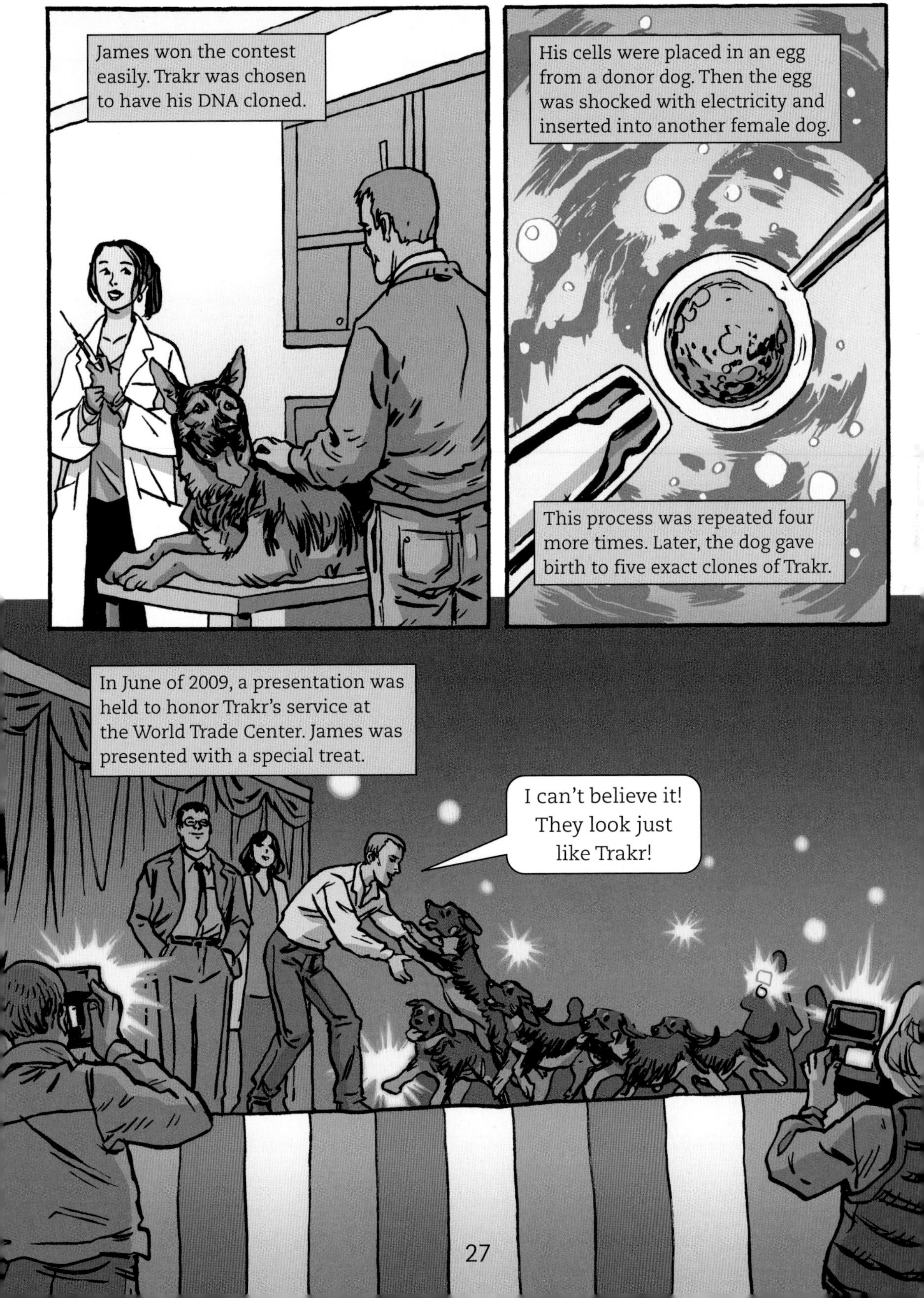
James won the contest easily. Trakr was chosen to have his DNA cloned.
His cells were placed in an egg from a donor dog. Then the egg was shocked with electricity and inserted into another female dog.
This process was repeated four more times. Later, the dog gave birth to five exact clones of Trakr.
In June of 2009, a presentation was held to honor Trakr's service at the World Trade Center. James was presented with a special treat.
I can't believe it! They look just like Trakr!

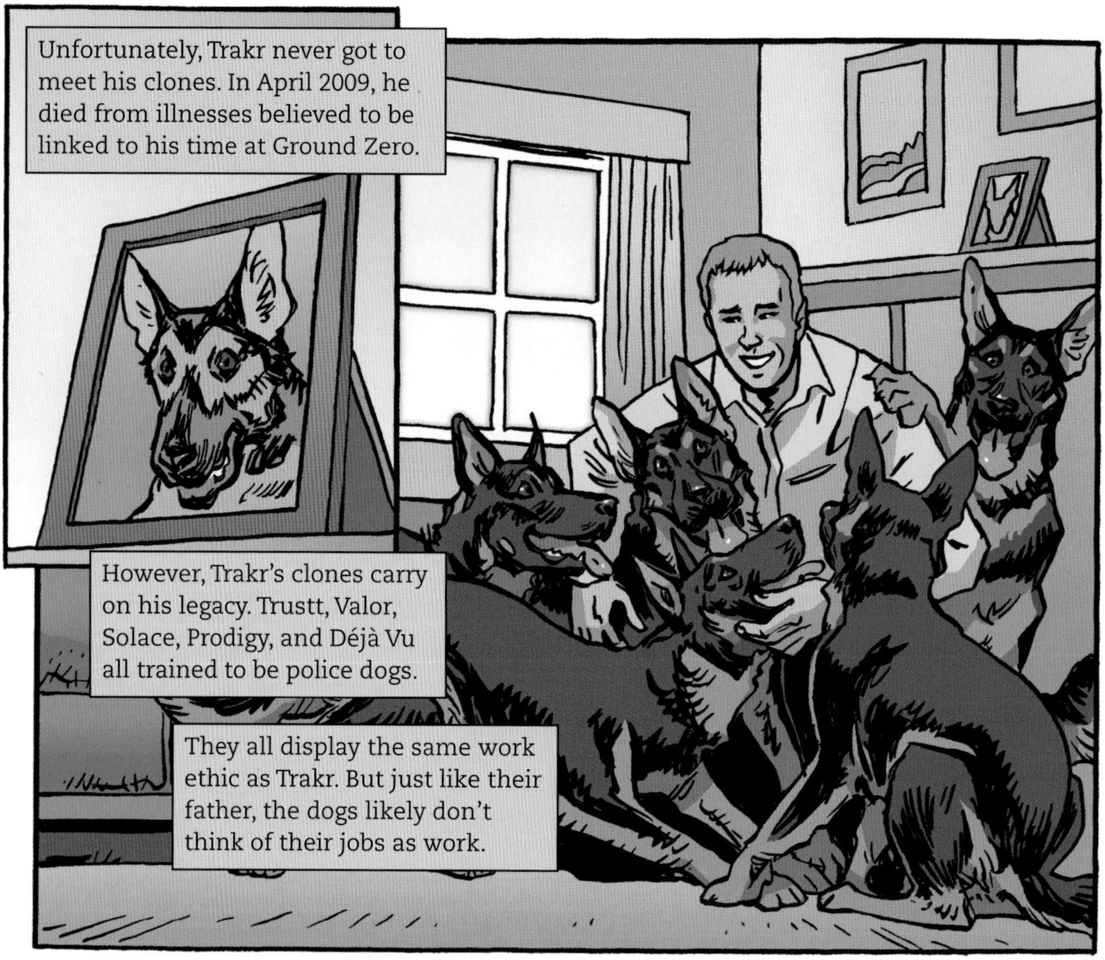
Unfortunately, Trakr never got to meet his clones. In April 2009, he died from illnesses believed to be linked to his time at Ground Zero.
However, Trakr's clones carry on his legacy. Trustt, Valor, Solace, Prodigy, and Déjà Vu all trained to be police dogs.
They all display the same work ethic as Trakr. But just like their father, the dogs likely don't think of their jobs as work.

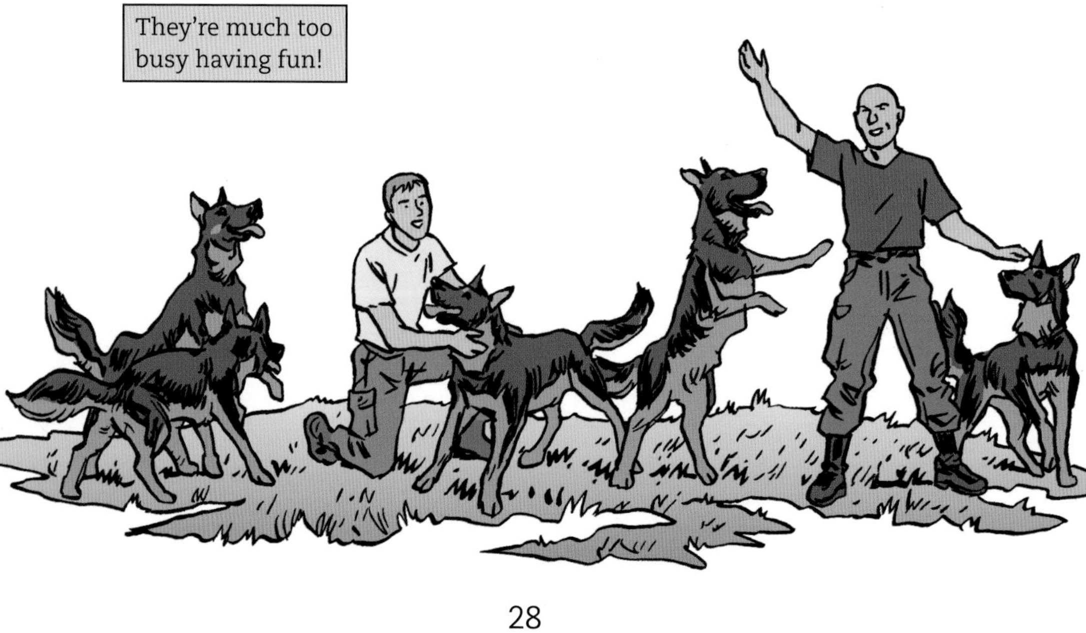
They're much too busy having fun!

Trakr Tales

In the years after the destruction of the World Trade Center, Trakr became famous for his work at Ground Zero. He was the subject of many books. In 2005, Jane Goodall honored Trakr and James Symington with the Extraordinary Service to Humanity Award. Trakr remained a popular public figure even after he died. In 2011, Time magazine named Trakr as one of its Top 10 Most Heroic Animals.

Trakr became famous for finding the last survivor in the rubble of the World Trade Center. But others say that honor belongs to a group of New York firefighters who prefer not to be publicized. Whatever the case, the heroism displayed during the days after the tragedy can't be understated. Trakr, James Symington, all the firefighters, rescue workers, and others who risked their lives to help others—they were all true heroes.

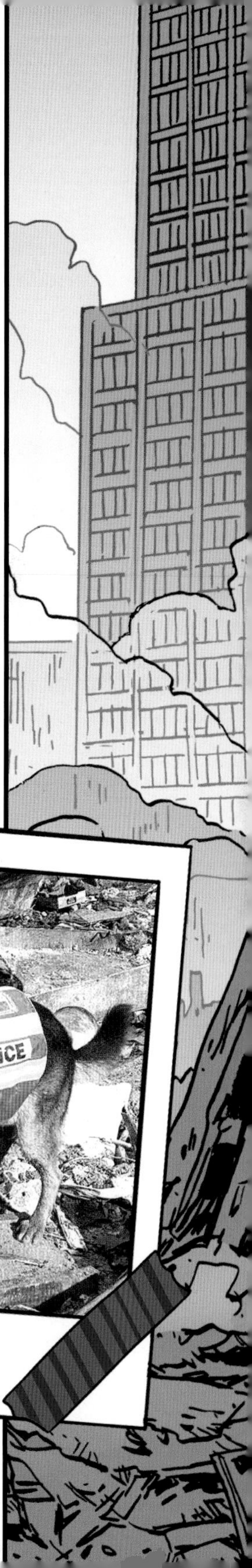

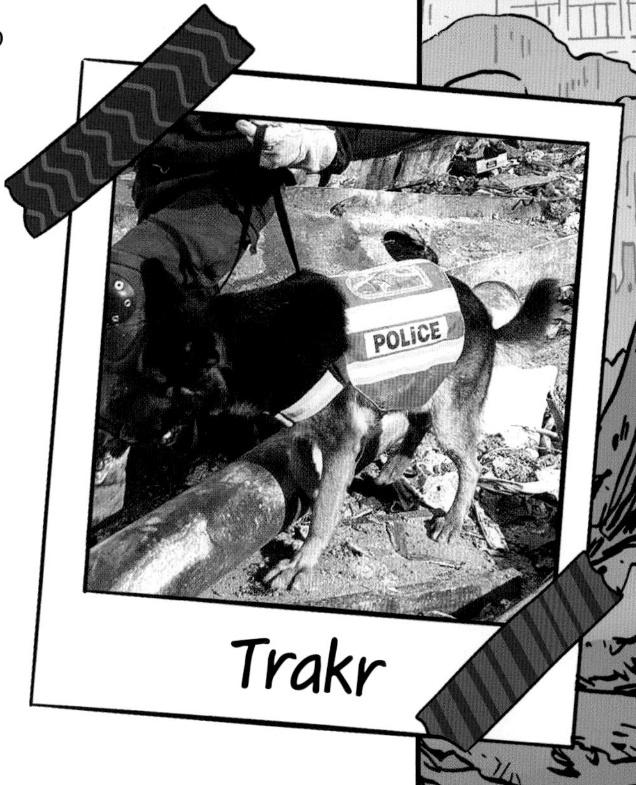
POLICE

Trakr

Glossary

authorized (AW-thuh-rahyzd)
having official authority or permission to do something

clone (KLOHN)
an organism with the exact same genes as the organism that produced it; the process of creating such an organism

debris (duh-BREE)
the scattered pieces of something that has been broken or destroyed

disability (dis-uh-BIH-luh-tee)
a physical or mental condition that prevents someone from performing normal daily tasks, usually caused by an illness, injury, or a condition at birth

DNA (dee-en-AY)
molecules inside the cells of living organisms that determine their characteristics; DNA stands for deoxyribonucleic acid

ferocious (fuh-ROH-shuhs)
fierce and savage

inhalation (in-huh-LEY-shuhn)
the action of breathing in

perp (PURP)
short for perpetrator; someone who commits a crime

work ethic (WURK ETH-ik)
a belief in the benefit and importance of work; willingness to work hard to achieve a task

Read More

Berglund, Bruce. *Togo Takes the Lead: Heroic Sled Dog of the Alaska Serum Run*. North Mankato, MN: Capstone, 2023.

Buckley Jr., James. *Canine Hero*. Minneapolis: Bearport Publishing Company, 2022.

Hamilton, Kimberlie. *Daring Dogs: 30 True Tales of Heroic Hounds*. New York: Scholastic Press, 2020.

Internet Sites

National Geographic Kids: Animal Heroes
kids.nationalgeographic.com/history/article/
animal-heroes

Newsweek: Amazing Rescues by Animals
newsweek.com/amazing-animals-343719

Top 10 Heroic Animals: Trakr the Dog
content.time.com/time/specials/packages/
article/0,28804,2059858_2059863_2060232,00.html

About the Author

Photo courtesy of
*Dorothy Manning
Photography*

Matthew K. Manning is the author of more than 100 books and dozens of comic books. Some of his favorite projects include the popular comic book crossover *Batman/ Teenage Mutant Ninja Turtles Adventures* and the 12-issue series *Marvel Action: Avengers* for IDW, *Exploring Gotham City* for Insight Editions, and the six-volume chapter book series Xander and the Rainbow-Barfing Unicorns for Capstone. Manning lives in Asheville, North Carolina with his wife, Dorothy, and their two daughters, Lillian and Gwendolyn. Visit him online at www.matthewkmanning.com.

About the Illustrator

Mark Simmons is a freelance illustrator and cartoonist based in San Francisco. His past work includes comics for publishers such as Capstone, Behrman House, and Rebellion, as well as animation and advertising storyboards, animated operas, and other strange things. He also teaches comic art, figure drawing, and wildlife illustration for local zoos, schools, and museums. He loves animals of all kinds, especially bugs! For more info, visit www.ultimatemark.com.